OSPREY AIRCRAFT OF THE ACES • 62

# Sopwith Triplane
# Aces of World War 1

SERIES EDITOR: TONY HOLMES

OSPREY AIRCRAFT OF THE ACES • 62

# Sopwith Triplane Aces of World War 1

Norman Franks

OSPREY
PUBLISHING

**Front cover**
**RNAS Flight Commander Roderic S Dallas DSC of 1 Naval Squadron flew Sopwith Triplane N5436 between late January and May 1917, achieving ten victories with it. After his first flight in this machine, he recorded in his log-book;**

**Tested oxygen set and went up to 26,000 ft – very curious sensation. I got drunk with the oxygen and could hardly recognise the country below me. I was frost bitten when coming down, and got it badly. This is the height record for the Triplane.'**

**Dallas' first victory (an LVG C observation aircraft) in N5436 came on 1 February, shortly after his unit had moved to the Somme front. He did not score again until 5 April, by which time 1 Naval Squadron had commenced operations in the build up to the Battle of Arras (launched four days later). Dallas fought with a formidable Albatros scout on this eve of battle patrol, and the action is depicted here in this cover artwork by Mark Postlethwaite. The Australian ace described the engagement in his log-book;**

**'We start the big show properly, and everybody is indeed a little anxious to see what things are really like. I lead the formation, Teddy (Gerrard) being good enough to come with me. As we climbed towards the lines, we felt secure, and were proud of our mounts. We soon got intimation that "Fritz" dwelt below, for from our high and lofty position we could look down with scorn on our baffled pursuers. Several Huns put themselves in our path, but we were cute and accepted not of their kind offer, till one, not knowing the sting in the "Tripod", fell victim to his horrid ways. We landed at Ham short of gas.'**

**Dallas claimed an Albatros D II scout 'out of control' in this action, the aircraft falling earthwards east of St Quentin at noon. Two more Albatros scouts (this time newer D IIIs) fell to him on 22 April, as he recounted in his log-book;**

**'Big scrap – met the "Travelling Circus" – and (Tom) Culling, my valiant comrade in the air, went with me into a formation of 14 of them. We revved around and counter-attacked, so to speak, and in the general mix-up Culling got one and I got two'**

First published in Great Britain in 2004 by Osprey Publishing
Elms Court, Chapel Way, Botley, Oxford, OX2 9LP

ISBN 1 84176 728 X

Edited by Tony Holmes and Bruce Hales-Dutton
Page design by Tony Truscott
Cover Artwork by Mark Postlethwaite
Aircraft Profiles by Harry Dempsey
Scale Drawings by Mark Styling
Index by Glyn Sutcliffe
Origination by Grasmere Digital Imaging, Leeds, UK
Printed through Bookbuilders in China

04 05 06 07 08    10 9 8 7 6 5 4 3 2 1

EDITOR'S NOTE
To make this best-selling series as authoritative as possible, the Editor would be interested in hearing from any individual who may have relevant photographs, documentation or first-hand experiences relating to the world's elite pilots, and their aircraft, of the various theatres of war. Any material used will be credited to its original source. Please contact Tony Holmes via e-mail at:
tony.holmes@osprey-jets.freeserve.co.uk

ACKNOWLEDGEMENTS
The Author wishes to thank the following individuals for their help with information and photographs – Mike Westrop, Stuart Leslie, Mike O'Connor, Tony Mellor-Ellis, Lucien Morareau, Phil Jarrett, Greg VanWyngarden, Frank Bailey and Graham Mottram. Thank you also to the RAF Museum for the provision of photographs.

For details of all Osprey Publishing titles please contact us at:

**Osprey Direct UK, P.O. Box 140, Wellingborough, Northants NN8 4ZA, UK**
E-mail: **info@ospreydirect.co.uk**

**Osprey Direct USA, c/o MBI Publishing, P.O. Box 1, 729 Prospect Ave, Osceola, WI 54020, USA**
E-mail: **info@ospreydirectusa.com**

Or visit our website: **www.ospreypublishing.com**

# CONTENTS

# TRIPLANE SCOUT

The only three-winged fighter aircraft to see active duty with Britain's flying services in World War 1, Sopwith's Triplane was the sole viable multi-winged aircraft design capable of challenging the biplane's supremacy during the early days of flight.

In terms of Sopwith lineage, the Triplane followed the $1^1/2$ Strutter two-seat all-purpose fighter, bomber and reconnaissance aircraft and the Pup single-seat scout. Like them, it carried just one forward-firing Vickers 0.303-in machine gun, synchronised to fire through the two

Following initial Admiralty trials and testing at RNAS Chingford, in Essex, prototype Sopwith Triplane, serialled N500, was sent on trial to 'A' Squadron, 1 Naval Wing, in Dunkirk in June 1916, where it was used by Australian R S Dallas in combat. The machine was also flown by other naval pilots who were keen to gain experience on the type. The scout was supplied to the RNAS in factory finish, including reflective underwing doping (*via T Mellor-Ellis*)

This photograph of N500 was taken not long after its arrival at St Pol, in France. The un-camouflaged scout was soon undergoing rigorous frontline trials with the RNAS. According to contemporary reports, N500 was ordered off against a suspected German aircraft within 15 minutes of being refuelled upon its arrival in France (*Bruce/Leslie*)

propeller blades. But by then Germans were already fielding fighters with twin machine guns, so from the start all three Sopwith types were out-gunned in the skies of France.

The Sopwith company passed its prototype Triplane for production as early as 28 May 1916, and although retaining the same armament as its forebears, it did have a more powerful engine in the form of a 110 hp Clerget 9Z rotary – the Pup relied on 80 hp Gnome or 100 hp Monosoupape motors. In order to test the new aircraft in combat conditions, prototypes were delivered to the Royal Naval Air Service (RNAS), which had generally used Sopwith machines in the early war years. Prototype N500 was sent to 'A' Naval Squadron (which would soon become 1 Naval Squadron), 1 Naval Wing, in Dunkirk, while second prototype N504 also went to France after being fitted with a 130 hp Clerget 9B.

The 130 hp Clerget engine replaced the manufacturer's early 110 hp rotary in production Triplanes from late 1916 onwards

N500 bore the brunt of some heavy handling in 1916, being tipped up on its nose on more than one occasion *(Bruce/Leslie)*

## RNAS UNIT NUMBERING

The system employed by the RNAS to identify its units at this time was described to the author some years ago by ranking naval ace, Canadian Ray Collishaw. In the period 1914-17, the RNAS was in an organisational mess. The highest operational unit was the wing captain's command, which was considered the equivalent to a battleship. Wing captains were allowed by the Admiralty to name squadrons as they liked. Sometimes, wing captains commanded as many as five or six stations, with squadrons at each one. Some allotted letters as the individual identifier for the unit, and their flights were in turn numbered. Other squadrons did the reverse, so it is hardly surprising that historians have become confused over the years.

When what became 8 Naval Squadron joined Royal Flying Corps (RFC) units on the Somme in October 1916, it was originally a lettered squadron with numbered flights. The RFC complained, and as a result the whole RNAS was reorganised to have consecutively numbered squadrons and lettered flights.

Triplane N500 arrived in France it its factory (un-camouflaged) finish in June 1916. When camouflage paint was applied some weeks later, the aircraft was adorned with the nickname *Brown Bread*, which referred to the colour of the PC10 khaki paint or dope applied to the scout's uppersurfaces, and had nothing to do with cockney rhyming slang, as has been suggested. It became a favourite of Flt

Sub-Lt R S Dallas, and on 1 July he encountered two German aircraft and was credited with forcing down an Aviatik C-type out of control.

Within weeks of his 25th birthday (30 July) when he claimed this victory, Australian Roderic Stanley Dallas hailed from Mount Stanley, in Queensland. He had enlisted in the Australian Army in 1913 and subsequently been commissioned, after which he applied for a transfer to the RFC when war came. Dallas was accepted by the RNAS instead, and he began flying training in June 1915. By December he was with 1 Naval Wing, piloting two-seaters and single-seat Nieuport scouts – Dallas claimed three combat victories in April and May 1916 flying the French fighter. The Australian's exposure to Triplane N500 came to a temporary halt, however, on 28 July when it was damaged by anti-aircraft fire and sent back to the Sopwith factory for new wings. The machine was back with Dallas by September, and on the 29th of that month he claimed an unidentified scout as destroyed, and having made a further Nieuport claim during July, this latest victory represented his sixth.

Dallas' impressions of the new Sopwith fighter had obviously been favourable, for orders were placed for an initial 40 Triplanes, followed soon afterwards by another 75. By this time the 130 hp Clerget had become its standard engine, and as Dallas and the RNAS test pilots had discovered, the combination of this motor and the Triplane's unique wing arrangement gave the machine a phenomenal rate of climb, exemplary manoeuvrability

Queenslander Roderic S Dallas poses for the camera in his distinctive RNAS uniform whilst undergoing training in late 1915 *(Franks collection)*

Now camouflaged in PC10 khaki and clear-doped undersides, N500 was sent from 'Naval 1' to 'Naval 5' to conduct further operational trials in early 1917 *(Andy Thomas)*

and a top speed of 120 mph (193 kmh) at 10,000 ft (3050 m). Despite its single gun armament, the Triplane's performance would help the RNAS combat the new German fighters which equipped the newly-formed *Jastas* now being encountered over the front.

The RFC also ordered the new machine, but with the arrival of the French SPAD VII (see *Aircraft of the Aces 39 - SPAD VII Aces of World War 1* for more details) it was agreed that the RNAS should have all the Triplanes, while the RFC would take the SPADs. In the event, while numbers 1, 8, 9, 10, 11 and 12 Naval Squadrons all showed Triplanes on strength, it was in fact only 1, 8, 9 and 10 Squadrons which used them in any numbers.

Flt Lt G M T Rouse ferried a number of Triplanes from England to 1 Naval Squadron, including N5450 on 14 February 1917. Note the manufacturer's decal on the 'Tripe's' propeller blade *(Bruce/Leslie)*

## —1 NAVAL SQUADRON—

1 Naval Squadron became fully equipped with Triplanes before the end of 1916, although it saw little action over the winter months from its base at Furnes, in Belgium – just along the coast from the Dunkirk airfields. This all changed in February 1917 when the RNAS was asked to continue assisting the RFC squadrons based further south, and the unit moved to Chipilly, south of Albert and east of Amiens. This was not exactly a new policy, for 8 Naval Squadron, with its Pups, had been helping the RFC on the Somme since October 1916, but had returned to St Pol in early February in order to re-equip with Triplanes. It was at this time that several RNAS units flew alongside the RFC on the British frontline running south from Ypres to Amiens. No sooner had 8 Naval Squadron started to receive its Triplanes

Triplane N5436 'C' in which Roderic Dallas scored 11 of his victories and fellow ace Cyril Ridley another two. This aircraft is also the subject of the book's cover artwork *(T Mellor-Ellis collection)*

than 9 and 10 Naval Squadrons also took delivery of the aircraft.

1 Naval Squadron's CO was Sqn Cdr F K Haskins, and under his leadership it achieved its first Triplane victories as February opened. Dallas was victorious again (in N5436), sending down an LVG C two-seater on the 1st. But it was April before the next success came his way. On the 5th Dallas claimed an Albatros scout out of control while flying N5436, and the next day three more Albatros fighters were sent spinning earthwards – one each by Dallas, B C Clayton and T G Culling. On the 8th, Dallas, who by this time had been awarded the Distinguished Service Cross (DSC), claimed an unidentified two-seater out of control east of Cambrai for his ninth kill.

Undergoing flying training at just 18 years of age, future ten-kill ace T F M 'Teddy' Gerrard eventually served with 1 Naval Squadron. He appears to be sat in a Maurice Farman MF 11 'shorthorn', which was widely used as a training platform in the early years of World War 1

The following day the Battle of Arras commenced. So too did 'Bloody April', a month that was to see the biggest Allied air losses in France so far.

The squadron was kept busy with patrols and escorts, despite poor weather, and on 14 April Flt Cdr T F N Gerrard made the next claim. This was his second victory, for he had previously enjoyed success flying a Nieuport while the unit was still designated 'A' Squadron.

Teddy Gerrard was the son of Brig Gen E L Gerrard DSO, and the youngster had joined the RNAS in 1915, aged 18. At one stage he had flown French-designed Franco British Aviation (FBA) flying boats from Dover, after which he had been transferred to 1 Wing . It was whilst flying Nieuports with the latter unit that Gerrard had claimed his first victory in July 1916. Most of his eight Triplane kills would be achieved in N5440, taking his overall score to ten. Gerrard would win the DSC and *Croix de Guerre* (CdG) and, in 1918, he flew briefly with No 208 Sqn and then commanded No 209 Sqn until war's end. Post-war, he flew a Sopwith Snipe in the Hendon Air Pageant in 1921, but was to die after a fall from his polo pony while serving in India.

The April 1917 battles saw Dallas, Culling and Gerrard among the scorers, and Flt Sub-Lts R P Minifie, F H M Maynard, H V Rowley and A P Haywood also made their first claims.

Thomas Grey Culling was born in New Zealand in May 1896, and had joined the RNAS in 1916. His six victories were scored between 6 April and 20 May 1917, all in N5444. Culling was awarded the DSC, but on 8 June, while flying N5491, he was shot down and killed by FlgMt H Bottler of *Marine Feld Jasta* (MFJ) I near Warneton.

Like Dallas, Richard Pearman Minifie was an Australian, born in Melbourne in February 1898 and living in Elsternwick, Victoria. Once in England he trained at Eastbourne, becoming a pilot in July 1916. Minifie too had gone to 1 Wing's 'A' Squadron, and once given a Triplane he began to score prolifically after his first two kills on 29 April 1917 – one of these (an Albatros D III) he shared with fellow Australian Triplane ace R A 'Bob' Little of 8 Naval Squadron. His first five claims came while

**Victorian Richard Minifie was 'Naval 1's' highest-scoring Triplane ace with 17 victories, beating fellow Australian R S Dallas by a single kill. The latter pilot's overall score easily beat Minifie's, however, Dallas claiming 32 kills as opposed to 21. However, both pilots' tallies (in Triplanes and overall) were beaten by ranking Australian ace R A Little of 'Naval 8', who claimed 24 and 47 victories respectively**

**Minifie scored two of his victories while flying N6303 in the summer of 1917** (Bruce/Leslie)

flying N5446, with ten more in N5454. In all, Minifie achieved 17 victories with the Triplane, plus four more flying the Camel. At 19, he was the war's youngest Australian ace.

Minifie was also one of the few to win three DSCs, the first being gazetted on 26 September 1917. A Bar followed on 16 November 1917 with the second awarded on 29 March 1918.

When Dallas left 1 Naval Squadron in early 1918, Minifie became the squadron's acting CO, pending the arrival of C D Booker. His luck ran out on 17 March 1918 when he came down near Houthulst Forest, probably after a fight with *Jasta* 47. Minifie was captured and spent the rest of the war in a prisoner of war (PoW) camp at Karlsruhe. Returning to Australia after his release, he later joined the family flour milling business, and in World War 2 served in the RAAF. Minifie died in March 1969.

## LOG-BOOKS

While researching this book, the author had access to the log-books of three Triplane aces, R A Little, R R Soar and W M Alexander. Despite reading many such log-books, he has rarely seen such descriptive action reports. Obviously the RNAS pilots were allowed a good deal more license in writing up their log-books, just as they were permitted to decorate their aircraft far more colourfully than their RFC compatriots. For example, Bob Little wrote of his 29 April action;

'1720 hrs. (N)5495. Time in the air 2 hours 15 mins. 15,000 ft. OP (Offensive Patrol). At about 1845 hrs I saw a red Albatros scout attack a BE near Monchy le Preux so I dived on the HA (hostile aircraft) and was followed by Flt Cdr Arnold and the remaining machines of our formation. Heavy AA fire was experienced and I lost sight of the HA. I observed our formation steering north and followed them. When over Drocourt I saw a formation of five Albatros scouts below our formation and at the same height as myself.

'I observed Flt Cdr Arnold dive down on them to about 6000 ft and then lost sight of him. I attacked them myself at the same time, and also saw Triplane 5446 (Flt Sub-Lt Minifie of 1 Naval Squadron) attacking them. We were going east towards Douai aerodrome and I passed a Triplane going west with three Albatros scouts close behind him. I think it had the number 16 on (its) fuselage. When over Douai aerodrome one of the Albatros scouts, which both I and Minifie were firing at, went down in a spin and I saw him crash on the aerodrome itself. The remaining HA continued to attack Triplane 5446 and, although he put up a splendid fight, was forced down by numbers to about 50 ft, where I last saw him. I was then attacked by more scouts.'

Later in life, Minifie noted;

'Yes, they nearly had me down on Douai aerodrome, about 200-300 ft off it. But luckily my Triplane was just that little shade faster than they were. I was going low for home, and they let me go and get a lead of about 500 yards on them. So that was that – they just couldn't catch me.'

Fellow Triplane ace Forster Herbert Martin Maynard was another New Zealander, born in May 1893. In 1914 he joined the Royal Navy Division before transferring to the RNAS the following year. An instructor before being posted to a Home Defence unit, it took Maynard some while to get to France, but once there he made his mark. His victory on 29 April 1917 was the first of six achieved that summer. Leaving 1 Naval Squadron in September, Maynard was sent to the Aircraft Depot at Dunkirk and, after recovering from a crash, he commanded a training depot. Remaining in the RAF post-war, Maynard retired in November 1945 as an air vice marshal, and holder of the Companion of the (Order of the) Bath and the Air Force Cross (AFC).

Soon after World War 1 Maynard attended RAF staff college, where he and others recorded their war experiences. He wrote;

'The Vickers gun on the Triplane was something quite new to many of us, and resulted in much time being spent on armament instruction. No Sopwith Triplane had (yet) fallen into German hands, and enemy machines did not appear at all anxious to come to grips with the new and rather mysterious scout. Whenever "Tripes" escorted 1½ Strutters on daylight raids no aerial opposition was ever encountered, and the enemy appeared to rely almost entirely for defence on numerous AA guns.

'OPs were carried out in pairs, but we hardly ever saw an enemy machine, and even if such a rarity did occur, the sight of a "Tripe" (which was easily identified from a long way off) was enough to send an enemy machine home. The moral

New Zealander Capt F H M Maynard claimed six kills while serving with '1 Naval'. He enjoyed a highly successful career in the RAF post-war *(Franks collection)*

**Below**
Triplane N534 was one of the few two-gun machines issued to '1 Naval', the scout being flown by aces Minifie, Dallas and Maynard. Indeed, the latter two each scored a single victory with it *(Bruce/Leslie)*

**Bottom**
Clearly not superstitious, Herbert Maynard was flying N5427 '13' when he scored his first victory on 29 April 1917 *(Bruce/Leslie)*

Triplane N5479 '8' was Herbert Maynard's most successful Triplane, the '1 Naval' pilot using it to claim three of his six victories in 1917 (Bruce/Leslie)

Another view of N5479, which was later re-numbered '18'. Future nine-kill ace J H Forman claimed his solitary Triplane victory while flying this aircraft on 18 October 1917, and a fifth victory was credited to the aircraft whilst being flown by a pilot named Cockey. This 'Tripe' was a presentation aircraft, being christened *Britons in Spain*

effect of this new type of machine was considerable at that time, and the Germans took a good deal of trouble over trying to blot us out.

'On 11 April 1917, the squadron moved to Bellevue aerodrome to take part in the Battle of Arras. German aircraft were plentiful over this section of the front, but it was some time before any of them would stay to fight with a "Tripe". When they did, however, which was only when considerably superior in numbers, we had fighting enough, and to spare. The Triplane was an excellent machine for fighting purposes, for although somewhat leisurely in manoeuvre, its extra-ordinarily good climbing powers generally enabled a good pilot to get the better of his opponent in an individual contest.

'About the middle of July I was given a two-gun Triplane to try out. The extra firepower afforded was, of course, extremely valuable. Unfortunately, the extra weight took off so much performance that the machine was no use in a formation of ordinary one-gun "Tripes". 1 Naval Squadron used two-gun "Tripes" against low-flying EA (Enemy Aircraft) two-seaters strafing frontline trenches at dawn or dusk, but it was difficult to identify enemy aircraft in poor light, while enemy crews could easily identify the three-wing Triplane.'

Like Maynard, fellow future RNAS ace Herbert Victor Rowley had also opened his account, in N5425, with an Albatros D III on 29 April 1917. Born in October 1897 in Crich, Derbyshire, he joined the RNAS on 30 April 1916 and learned to fly at Chingford, in Essex, where he duly received his 'ticket' on 24 August. Sent to 1 Naval Squadron in February 1917, Rowley would go on to score five victories with the Triplane – all in different aircraft – and then take his score to nine as a Camel flight commander.

Unknown to him, Rowley was responsible for wounding the German ace Kurt Wolff, leader of *Jasta* 11, on 11 July 1917. 1 Naval Squadron and JG I (*Jastas* 4, 6, 10 and 11, which comprised the 'Richthofen Circus') flew opposite each other throughout that month, and as will be mentioned later, *Jasta* 11 downed three of the unit's Triplanes on 7 July, including Cyril Eyre – Wolff achieved his 33rd, and final, victory in that fight. Four days later, 1 Naval Squadron again tangled with *Jastas* 4 and 11, and Wolff was wounded in the hand from a burst of fire from Rowley. The German ace broke off the action and flew home, only to crash-land on the railway line running close to *Jasta* 11's base at Marckebeke, near Kortrijk (Courtrai). Oddly, Rowley received no decorations for his war service. He remained in the RAF post-war, becoming a wing commander in 1937, and World War 2 he served in the Far East as an air commodore.

Dusting themselves off from the trials and tribulations of 'Bloody April', the pilots of 1 Naval Squadron continued to assist the RFC over the Western Front. Minifie, Culling, Dallas and Gerrard regularly added to their scores during this period, with Teddy Gerrard claiming a double on 4 June during an exceptionally busy day for the RNAS and RFC.

Shortly before 0800 hrs on the 4th, ten Triplanes had engaged a large formation of German scouts, and in the ensuing air battle Nieuport scouts and some SE 5s had also joined in. A number of 1 Naval Squadron's aces were involved, including Minifie, Rowley, Ridley, Maynard and Gerrard, and the latter pilot sent a German machine spinning earthwards. He then shared in the destruction of a second scout, which was seen to crash. Gerrard's first Albatros had been on the tail of a Nieuport, and the second, which, he noted had a black fuselage and two white bands around it, was attacking Flt Sub-Lt L H Cockey. This aircraft was also attacked by the Nieuport scout of Capt P F Fullard of No 1 Sqn RFC, the shared victory being his fourth of an eventual 40.

Amongst the German fighter force encountered on the morning of 4 June were Albatros scouts from *Jasta* 18, several of whom succeeded in putting bullets into Gerrard's Triplane, shooting away his lateral controls. Later, his machine – N5440 – was described as 'riddled'. However, he and Fullard had knocked down Ofstv Matthias Dennecke, who died in hospital the following day.

H V Rowley of 'Naval 1' scored five victories flying Triplanes and four more in Camels *(Franks collection)*

Triplane pilots of 1 Naval Squadron pose for a group shot at Bailleul aerodrome in July 1917. They are, from left to right, S M Kinkead DSC (6 kills on Triplanes and 35 overall), J H Forman (1 kill on Triplanes and 9 overall), H Wallace, A G A Spence (6 kills on Triplanes and 9 overall), H L Everitt, H V Rowley (5 kills on Triplanes and 9 overall), Luard, Magrath, E D Crundell (3 kills on Triplanes and 7 overall), W H Sneath, Burton, A R McAfee, S W Rosevear (8 kills on Triplanes and 25 overall), R P Minifie (17 kills on Triplanes and 21 overall), R S Dallas (16 kills on Triplanes and 32 overall), C B Ridley (4 kills on Triplanes and 11 overall), J S deWilde, White and E B Holden *(Bruce/Leslie collection)*

The grave of six-kill ace C A Eyre of 1 Naval Squadron at Pont-du-Hem Cemetery in France. He was shot down on 7 July 1917, aged 21. The headstone also records the loss of Flt Sub-Lt E G A Eyre, aged 19, of 'Naval 4', shot down by 44-kill ace Bruno Loerzer of *Jasta* 26 on 21 October 1917. E G A Eyre has no known grave *(N Franks)*

Cyril Askew Eyre opened his account on 4 May 1917 by shooting down an Albatros. Born in April 1896, and a graduate of Magdalen College in Oxford, he had joined the RNAS in Toronto, Canada, in 1915. By the summer of 1916 Eyre was flying Pups with 'A' Squadron, and this was his first confirmed success. He went on to claim six victories by 3 July 1917. However, on the 7th he was piloting one of two Triplanes (N6291) claimed by *Jasta* 11, Eyre being brought down by Ltn Alfred Niederhoff. This was the German's fourth of his eventual seven victories, although he was not to survive the month either. Kurt Wolff shot down the other Triplane, flown by Flt Sub-Lt H K Millward (N6309), who was also killed. He had become the German ace's 33rd, and last, victim.

1 Naval Squadron managed to bring down another German machine behind Allied lines on 27 May, this being Flt Sub-Lt D W Ramsey's first, and only, victory. Flying N5480, his opponent was an Albatros scout, although there appears no record of it either being lost or captured. Possibly the pilot landed in the trenches and managed to reach his own lines. Ramsey was killed in this same Triplane over Dadizeele on 27 July by Vfw Freidrich Altemeier of *Jasta* 24.

The established Triplane aces continued to score during May, June and July, and on the seventh day of the latter month a future ace downed his first opponent. Flt Sub-Lt Anthony George Allen Spence was born in Toronto, Canada, in May 1897. Having attended Toronto University to gain a Batchelor of Arts degree, he was another who joined the RNAS in Canada (in November 1916) and ended up with 1 Naval Squadron in 1917. By the end of July Spence had scored three victories, and by the time the Camels arrived his total had doubled. Wounded on 8 November, he recovered to claim three more kills with the Camel, taking

Capt C B Ridley DSC of 1 Naval Squadron, who finished the war with 11 victories to his credit, four of them on Triplanes
*(Bob Lynes collection)*

Cyril Ridley was flying '14' (believed to be N5437) when he scored his first victory on 29 April 1917. He shared this kill with fellow future ace H V Rowley
*(Bob Lynes collection)*

his final tally to nine. Spence then returned to England to become an instructor.

In August 1917 two more new aces emerged from within the ranks of 1 Naval Squadron – Flt Lt C B Ridley and Flt Sub-Lt S W Rosevear. Although born in Britain in January 1895, Cyril Burfield Ridley was also living in Toronto when war broke out. Joining the RNAS and flying with 1 Naval Squadron, he shared a kill on 29 April 1917, gained his third on 14 August and claimed a fourth on 10 September. By July 1918 Ridley had increased his score to 11, although seven of these had been achieved in Camels. Sadly, he did not live long to celebrate the peace that he had helped to win for he perished in a flying accident in Cologne, Germany, in May 1920.

Yet another Canadian, Stanley Wallace Rosevear was born in Walkerton, Ontario, on 9 March 1896 and lived in Port Arthur. He studied at Toronto University and joined the RNAS on 19 January 1917. After training, Rosevear was sent to Dover in June, and on 14 August (in N6299) brought down his first hostile aircraft – an Albatros D V, which crashed north-east of Ypres. Rosevear scored three more victories in this machine, and another four in N5489. With the arrival of the Camel, he really began to score, so that by the end of April 1918 his victory tally had reached an impressive 25 – all in just 15 months since joining the colours. Rosevear won the DSC and Bar, but on 25 April he failed to pull his Camel out of a dive during shooting practice (surely unnecessary?) against a ground target, and he died of the injuries he sustained in the subsequent crash in No 19 Casualty Clearing Station.

The only other Triplane ace to emerge in 1 Naval Squadron during the summer of 1917 was the amazing Samuel Marcus Kinkead. Hailing from Johannesburg, South Africa, 'Kink' was born in February 1897

**Canadian S W Rosevear of 1 Naval Squadron scored his first eight (of 25) victories while flying Triplanes. His remaining kills were claimed on the Camel**

**This particular aircraft (N5420) was the very first production-standard Triplane to be built by Sopwith. Issued to 'Naval 1' in the autumn of 1916, the scout did not remain in this condition for very long, as it was damaged beyond repair on 14 December 1916 *(via Andy Thomas)***

South African S M 'Kink' Kinkead DSO DSC and Bar DFC and Bar (foreground) gained six of his 35 victories flying Triplanes with 1 Naval Squadron. He is seen here with E V Reid whilst serving with DH 9-equipped No 47 Sqn in White Russia in 1919. The unit received Camels soon after this photograph was taken *(Franks collection)*

and joined the RNAS in September 1915. His first posting was to the Dardanelles with 3 Naval Wing, where he was reported to have scored three kills with Bristol and Nieuport scouts

By the autumn of 1916 Kinkead had returned to England and been posted to Dunkirk, from where, in mid 1917, he moved to 1 Naval Squadron. Victory number four, and his first with the Triplane, came on 17 September, and number five followed exactly one month later. By 12 November Kinkead's score had risen to nine, six of which he had claimed with the Triplane. The last – a Pfalz D III – was shared with Flt Sub-Lt J H Forman, who was flying in Camel B5651, (one of the unit's first examples). All six of Kinkead's Triplane claims were made in N5465.

Kinkead continued to fly with 1 Naval Squadron – later No 201 Sqn after the establishment of the RAF on 1 April 1918 – until the end of August 1918, by which time his score had increased to 32. He received the DSC and Bar and DFC and Bar, to which he added the DSO for service in Russia in 1919-20. Flying with No 47 Sqn RAF against the Bolsheviks, he had shot down a number of Russian aircraft, and later saw action policing Mesopotamia and Kurdistan. Kinkead was killed in a flying accident in March 1928 whilst practising with the RAF Schneider Trophy Team.

In all, 1 Naval Squadron produced nine Triplane aces, whilst two future aces started their scoring runs during the unit's successful association with Sopwith's three-winged fighter. They, and several pilots who scored the odd victory, accounted for well over 100 German aircraft destroyed or sent down out of control between January and mid-November 1917.

As Ray Collishaw told the author;

'"Naval 1" was the first Sopwith Triplane squadron, and it went down to the Somme early in 1917 to join the RFC. In early June the squadron moved to the Ypres Front, where the heaviest and most intense air fighting of the war occurred. Unfortunately for "Naval 1", it was kept too long equipped with Triplanes, and so suffered heavy casualties. The outstanding people in the squadron at that time were Kinkead, Gerrard, Dallas, Rosevear, Ridley and Minifie.'

## SQUADRON MARKINGS

Individual Triplanes were typically identified by a large white number – from 1 to 18 – painted mid-way along the fuselage, and no roundels were carried on the fuselage sides. There were exceptions though, with R S Dallas' N5436 featuring a white 'C' on its fuselage, as well as a roundel. A number of machines also had had white or beige wheel covers. As more official, and permanent, squadron markings came into force on 26 August 1917, 1 Naval Squadron adorned its Triplanes with two small white vertical bars painted just aft of the individual fuselage number. Some aircraft had their individual number repeated on the top fuselage decking, such as N5377 '4'. A handful also featured personal names beneath the cockpit, such as N5387 '15' *PEGGY*.

## WHAT WAS THE TRIPLANE LIKE TO FLY?

The Fall 1971 edition of the Canadian Aviation Historical Society's journal contained the transcript of a talk given by Wg Cdr Paul Hartman RCAF (Rtd) in 1968 at the International Conference, recorded by K M Molsen, about flying vintage aircraft. The wing commander related his experiences at the controls of several World War 1 aircraft, and of the reproduction Sopwith Triplane built by Carl Swanson, which he flew at RCAF Station Rockcliffe, in Ottawa. He said;

'Of all the vintage aircraft flown by us in 1917, this was undoubtedly the most pleasant to fly. It possessed stability and control response so good as to be unique, not only for aircraft of that era but also in comparison with many of today's machines. Its positive stability about all three axes, plus a horizontal stabiliser that was adjustable by the pilot

**Clayton & Shuttleworth-built Triplane N5387 '15' was nicknamed *PEGGY* by 1 Naval Squadron after being passed on to the RNAS following service with the French, and leading ace Charles Nungesser. Parked behind it the hangar is N5425 '16', which was flown on occasion by aces Rosevear and Rowley (Franks collection)**

during flight, resulted in an aircraft that could be flown with a minimum of concentration and effort. Indeed, when the aircraft was properly rigged and correctly trimmed in flight, it could be flown hands-off. The controls were light, powerful and well-harmonised and the aircraft's response to the controls was excellent.

'As I settled into the seat for the first flight, I was again struck by the simplicity of the cockpit and the paucity of instrumentation. The latter consisted of an airspeed indicator and altimeter, with a tachometer and pulsometer providing means of monitoring engine operation and performance. Flight and engine controls were almost identical to those in the Nieuport – a throttle, Tampier lever, fuel cock and "blip" switch for engine control, plus the usual control stick and rudder bar. A dual magneto system provided somewhat more insurance against an ignition system malfunction than was the case in the Nieuport.

'The seat was much lower in the Triplane than in other aircraft, and my immediate impression on sitting in it for the first time was of very limited visibility forward through an arc of about 30 degrees either side of the centre line. However, a gap between the wing root of the centre mainplane and the fuselage side enabled the pilot to see forward and downward for the approach and landing. The single, cowl-mounted Vickers machine gun was removed for the first test flight. The combination of a breech block projecting well aft into the cockpit – within six to eight inches of my face – and the ever-present possibility of my botching the first landing and flipping the aircraft onto its nose dictated its removal. I had no desire to lose a mouthful of teeth!

'The engine was primed, throttle and Tampier levers set, switch on. Contact! The engine fired immediately and settled into the rhythmic rattle typical of the rotary and idled smoothly at about 700 rpm. It was difficult to get a precise reading of the revs because, although the engine was of British manufacture, the tachometer was a French instrument that gave slightly erratic readings of twice-actual engine speed. I had no

**Marked with a white '7', this 'Naval 1' Triplane bore the name *KAMSIT* or *KAMBRIT* immediately below the cockpit, although it is only visible on the original print of this photograph *(T Mellor-Ellis)***

intention of allowing this aircraft to become airborne in a three-point attitude, as happened during my first flight in the Nieuport. Thus the control stick was held about one inch forward of centre as I opened the throttle.

'The ship accelerated quickly, as the power was increased to approximately 1150 rpm, and the tail rose at about 20 knots. There was almost no tendency for the aircraft to swing to the left due either to torque or the gyroscopic effects of the engine, and very little rudder was required to keep the aircraft straight during the take-off run.

'With the tail up and the aircraft in almost a level flight attitude, visibility over the nose during the take-off run was excellent. At 38 to 40 knots, the aircraft left the ground and accelerated rapidly to 60 knots. I eased it into a climb, holding the speed constant at 60. The altimeter indicated 650 to 700 ft as the aircraft boundary was crossed – a distance of approximately 5000 ft from the take-off point. I had been airborne less than a minute at that instant, so the aircraft had a fair rate of climb. Those watching on the ground told me later it appeared to be climbing like a homesick angel. It certainly felt so to me. I continued the climb to 900 ft, where I levelled off and made a left hand turn to return to the field.

'During the turn, with an angle of bank of about 40 degrees, I became aware that a coordinated entry into the turn had been made without my being aware of it. There was no slip or skid, and no gyroscopic precession was apparent from the engine. The wind blasting squarely into my face confirmed the former, and the necessity to hold a very light top rudder force during the turn attested to the latter.

'At 1500 ft above the aerodrome a stall check was made. The throttle was closed and the engine idled at approximately 700 rpm at an

1 Naval Squadron line-up in full strength at Bailleul in 1917, with Richard Minifie's N5454 – previously 'Naval 8's *HILDA* – parked in the foreground. Minifie scored ten victories while flying this machine. White-finned Triplane N5472 '17' was H V Rowley's aircraft in late 1917

**Early Triplane master 'Reggie' Dallas poses with his brand new Sopwith scout in France in late 1916 (Bruce/Leslie)**

indicated airspeed of 40 knots. The control stick was fully back. The aircraft was hanging on the propeller in a 12- to 13-degree nose high attitude, refusing to stall. I depressed the blip switch, the rpm decreased, and the nose dropped. The ailerons were fully effective immediately prior to either wing drop. As the nose dropped, the blip switch was released and the engine picked up to idle rpm. The height lost during recovery from the stall was 75 ft.

After recovering from the stall, the aircraft was trimmed to glide at 50 knots. The gliding angle and speed were held reasonably constant by continuous use of the blip switch to reduce the engine rpm at idle. The aircraft would not descend to an acceptable speed or angle of descent unless the engine power was reduced below its normal idling range by constant, regular interruption of the ignition. Care had to be taken to ensure that the duration of ignition cut did not exceed four to five seconds.

'An old RAF manual describing the idiosyncrasies of the rotary engine warned that cutting the ignition for prolonged periods of time without turning off the main fuel cock was to be avoided because a combusting mixture of air and fuel could accumulate in the engine cowling with surprising and, on occasion, catastrophic results when the ignition was eventually turned (back) on.

'The glide was continued to 1000 ft, where the engine power was set at 1100 rpm and a level speed run made. Subsequent corrections for temperature showed the aircraft achieved a true air speed of 111 mph. This figure agreed with performance figures quoted for the aircraft in 1917/18. The speed run also enabled a last check to be made of the effectiveness of the adjustable horizontal stabiliser as a trimming device. The control for changing the stabiliser angle was a wheel about ten inches in diameter mounted on the right side of the cockpit, level with, and slightly forward of, the pilot's elbow. Movement of the wheel through an arc of about five to six inches changed the stabiliser angle about one degree. It was a positive and powerful trimming device.

'A speed of 105 knots indicated was the maximum to which the aircraft was flown. It displayed a slight tendency to yaw to the left as speed increased in a dive, then yaw to the right as speed was reduced. The yaw was easily overcome with rudder. The landing was straightforward and easy. The aircraft was glided at 50 knots to a height about 15 ft above the ground, at which point the blip switch was depressed and held. The control stick was eased slowly rearward to flare the aircraft. It slowly lost height as the speed decreased during the flare, until the aircraft was about one foot off the ground at a speed of about 40 knots. Stick fully back at this point – a slight sinking feeling as the air speed needle touched 37 to 38 knots – and we're on the ground!'

As naval fighter pilots found in 1917, the Triplane was generally 15 mph faster than the German Albatros D III fighter, and the Sopwith machine could both out-climb and out-turn it.

# 'NAVAL 8'

The RNAS's 8 Naval Squadron began to equip with Sopwith Triplanes in February 1917, the unit having formed at St Pol, near Dunkirk, in October 1916 with elements drawn from 1, 4 and 5 Naval Wings. Its primary mission was to help the hard-pressed RFC squadrons based at Vert Galand, mid way between Amiens and Doullens, the naval unit flying Nieuport scouts, Sopwith two-seat $1^1/2$ Strutters and eventually some Pups. Moving back to the French coast to work up on the Triplane, 'Naval 8' returned to the frontline in March with a move to Auchel, west of Béthune. It then moved to St-Eloi, north-west of Arras, where the pilots had a fabulous landmark in the shape of the old monastery ruins atop nearby Mount St-Eloi.

8 Naval Squadron had relieved 'Naval 10', also Triplane-equipped, at the front, coming under the control of the RFC's No 10 Wing of No 1 Brigade at the same time. Bad weather kept the newcomers on the ground until 5 April – four days before the Battle of Arras was due to commence. The unit's CO was Sqn Cdr G R Bromet, who later became Air Vice Marshal Sir Geoffrey Bromet DSO OBE *Légion d'Honneur* (Ld'H).

Although the weather remained poor, future high-scoring ace Flt Cdr R J O Compston did succeed in taking the fight to the Germans on the 5th in Triplane N5471, claiming a Halberstadt scout sent down 'out of control'.

Robert John Orton Compston was born in England in January 1898, the son of a vicar. He was just 17 when he joined the RNAS in 1915. Compston initially carried out Home Defence duties, but he was soon posted to France, and 8 Naval Squadron, in late 1916. He gained one victory flying a Nieuport scout in December and doubled his tally with his 5 April claim. Compston would achieve a high score (25), many of them with the Triplane, before moving onto Camels. He would receive the DSC and two Bars and later the DFC.

Two days later Flt Sub-Lt R A Little, in N5469, destroyed another Halberstadt, and Flt Lt C D Booker claimed an Albatros scout.

As mentioned earlier, Bob Little's flying log-book survives, and as he wrote such interesting accounts of his aerial battles, many are worth noting. So far he had achieved four victories with Sopwith Pups, so this 7 April evening combat was his fifth;

'When near Arras at 7000 ft I observed two machines about the same height as myself being fired at by AA. I proceeded to attack one of the machines, which was bright red with blue wings. I noticed tracer passing between his planes and he dived away. At the same time I was attacked from the beam by a machine of similar type, but coloured green. I out-manoeuvred him and drove him down in a steep spiral, firing at him all the time. Then, from a height of 2000 ft, I saw him fly into the ground near the trenches north-east of Arras. I was then attacked from above and my machine was hit in several places, including the oil tank. I climbed away to 10,000 ft and returned home.'

8 Naval Squadron's R J O Compston DSC and two Bars DFC scored nine victories while flying Triplanes and ended the war with a total of 25 *(Franks collection)*

The reported Halberstadt was more likely an Albatros, which went down at 1930 hrs and was credited to Little by the RFC. Confirmation often came from anti-aircraft batteries just behind the frontlines or observers in the trenches. Following this early evening scrap, a British Third Army AA position reported;

'At 6:45 pm on 7/4/17 a Sopwith Triplane, working alone, attacked 11 hostile machines, almost all Albatros scouts, north-east of Arras. He completely outclassed the whole patrol of hostile machines, diving through them and climbing above them. One Albatros scout, painted red, which had been particularly noticed by this section, dived on to him and passed him. The Sopwith dived on him and then easily climbed again above the whole patrol, drawing them all the time towards the anti-aircraft guns. As soon as they were within range, the anti-aircraft guns opened fire on the patrol, which turned eastwards, and the Sopwith returned safely. The officers who witnessed the combat report that the manoeuvring of the Sopwith Triplane completely outclassed that of the Albatros scout.'

Robert Alexander Little was an Australian, born in Hawthorn, Melbourne on 19 July 1895. His parents were Scottish, although they had moved to Canada before emigrating to Australia. Little was 20 when he joined the RNAS in 1915, having sailed to England to take private flying lessons, which he completed at Hendon at the end of October. Based at Dunkirk, he flew several different types on operations before the Pups arrived. Little's first two victories once he had joined 'Naval 8' came in November 1916, with a third in December and a fourth in January. He would eventually become one of the top fighter aces of the war, and the ranking Australian ace, and he would score 24 kills with the Triplane. Prior to his death in action in May 1918, Little would achieve 47 victories and be awarded the DSO and Bar and DSC and Bar.

Little's log-book records the following entry for 24 April 1917;

'Triplane N5469, 1230 hrs. On the report of a hostile machine coming towards the aerodrome, I was sent up to engage it. I met the HA flying east over Auchel aerodrome at 12,000 ft. I dived and attacked it. I saw two Nieuport scouts also diving to attack it. The

'Naval 8's' top ace was Australian R A Little DSO DSC with 24 victories. By the time of his death in action on the night of 27 May 1918 his score had risen to 47 (Franks collection)

**The DFW C V of FA 18, brought down by Little on 24 April 1917**

**C D Booker, right, was second top-scoring 'Naval 8' Triplane ace with 21 kills. He is seen here with 'Naval 4's' ace A M Shook** *(Bruce/Leslie)*

German pilot turned north and I followed him, firing whenever an opportunity offered itself. I noticed the observer was not returning the fire, so I closed in on him. He was losing height all the time, and when a mile east of Béthune, I observed my tracers going into his fuselage. I was then firing at a range of 10 to 15 yards. He then nose-dived and I dived after him. He landed in a field, and I was unable to get my engine going after the dive and had to land alongside the HA. I ran into a ditch and turned over. I got out of my machine and went across to the Germans and took them prisoner. The pilot, Ltn Neumuller (and observer Ltn Huppertz) told me he knew he would never get back when he saw me coming to attack him.'

Friedrich Neumuller and Hans Huppertz were serving with *Fliegerabteilung* Nr 18 when forced down in their DFW C V, the latter being captured intact and receiving the RFC captured aircraft number G24.

The story goes that as Little crawled out of his 'Tripe' to claim his prisoners, Neumuller saluted smartly and said in English, 'It looks as if I have brought you down, not you me, doesn't it?' Apparently, the German crew had been taking photographs of the airfield at St-Eloi and the area around Béthune. During the battle the observer had got himself entangled in his machine gun's ammunition belt, and Little and Neumuller had to free him.

It may well be that Little had decided to land, not so much due to his engine trouble, but because he was

N5482 *MAUD* was used by C D Booker to claim no fewer than 17 of his 21 Triplane victories. The zig-zag bands around the fuselage were red, white and blue in colour *(Bruce/Leslie)*

Triplane N6290, which was later named *DIXIE,* was flown by ace A R Arnold during its service with 'Naval 8'. He scored his fourth and fifth victories while flying this machine in the early summer of 1917 *(Bruce/Leslie)*

eager to claim his prisoners in person, especially as most combats took place over enemy-held territory where there were no opportunities to do so. It is possible that in the excitement he might well have misjudged his landing area and hence ended up in the ditch. The Nieuport scouts were from No 40 Sqn, and Lt I P R Napier, together with Lt Brevis, shared in the victory. It was Ian Napier's second of an eventual 12 kills, and he would receive the Military Cross (MC) and French Ld'H and CdG.

'Naval 8' was to produce several exceptional aces in 1917, one of whom was Flt Lt C D Booker. He downed an LVG two-seater on 14 April for his second Triplane victory, and his third kill overall. Born in April 1897 and hailing from Speldhurst, in Kent, Charles Dawson Booker spent much of his early life in Australia, where he attended Melbourne School. Returning to England in 1911 with his parents, he lived in Tunbridge Wells and completed his education at Bedford School, joining the RNAS in September 1915.

Booker initially flew with 5 Wing, before transferring to the newly-formed 8 Naval Squadron and scoring his first victory in a Pup in January 1917. Before April was out, he had raised his score to five, a figure he would almost triple in May.

In his diary, E D Crundell described Booker, who was his flight commander, as;

'. . . a little fellow, usually very silent, who fears nothing, but he would run a mile from any girl because he feels so shy in their company. He runs "C" Flight most efficiently. He says he hopes the war will go on for ever because he loves air fighting, and if the war were to end he is afraid he might not be able to find a suitable job.'

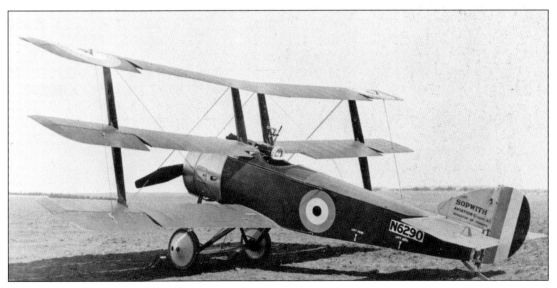

Booker was a brave and resourceful pilot, but he was not invincible. During a fight on 11 August 1917 he was shot up and actually claimed as a victory by *Jasta* 12's Viktor Schobinger (his second kill of a final tally of eight). However, Booker coaxed his 'Tripe' *MAUD* (N5482) back over the lines, where he force-landed near Farbus.

One week later he increased his score to 22 (21 on Triplanes), and in March 1918 he was made CO of Camel-equipped No 201 Sqn. Booker had taken his tally to 29 by the time he was killed in action on 13 August in a fight with JG II. He was on patrol with a new pilot when both Camels were attacked by numerous Fokker D VIIs. Booker fought a tremendous action, but in securing the escape of his tyro wingman he himself fell to the German ace Ulrich Neckel, *Staffelführer* of *Jasta* 19. He had become the German's 22nd victory out of an eventual total of 30.

Flt Lt A R Arnold, in N5458, downed an Albatros scout on 21 April 1917 and shared in the capture of a second fighter (flown by Ltn Gustav Nerst of *Jasta* 30) with a No 25 Sqn FE 2b RFC crew. D III 2147/ 17 came down behind British lines at Oppy, close to Arras. Nerst, who had three kills (two scored with *Jasta* 10), died in the crash, the wreckage of which became G 22 in the British serial number listing of hostile aircraft downed over Allied lines.

Anthony Rex Arnold, usually known as Rex, was born in August 1896 and came from Fareham, Hampshire. Joining the RNAS in 1916, he flew on Home Defence duties until his posting to France, where he found himself with 'Naval 8'. He would gain five victories by mid-June 1917 and win the DSC. After service as an instructor in England, Arnold was given command of the RAF's No 79 Sqn in June 1918. He received the DFC whilst leading this unit mostly for his ground attack work, and also added the Belgian CdG to his list of decorations. Post-war, Arnold remained in the RAF and became a group captain in 1936 as Senior Air Staff Officer of 24 Group.

Flt Sub-Lt G G Simpson was another future ace to make his first Triplane claims (he already had one on a Pup) in April 1917, getting kills on the 24th and 26th of that month. George Goodman Simpson called himself a Londoner, although he was actually born in Australia in September 1896. He joined the RNAS in August 1915 and served with 1 Naval Wing, before joining 'Naval 8'. By the end of May he had

Flt Lt Rex Arnold DSC (later Maj Arnold DSC DFC, OC of No 79 Sqn RAF) scored five victories flying Triplanes in 1917 *(Franks collection)*

Flt Cdr G G Simpson DSC gained eight victories, seven of which claimed flying Triplanes between April and July 1917 *(Franks collection)*

An official portrait of 'Naval 8's' leading ace, Bob Little *(Franks collection)*

achieved six victories (five with the Triplane) and been awarded the DSC. Simpson then went to 9 Naval Squadron, where he added two more Triplane kills in July. He later flew on Home Defence sorties from Cranwell in late 1917, before becoming a test pilot at Martlesham Heath in 1918.

A further extract from Bob Little's log-book for 30 April 1917 reads;

'Triplane N5493, 0630 hrs, special mission. At 0645 hrs, east of Arras, I observed three FEs fighting with five Albatros scouts. I dived on the HA and started manoeuvring for position when I saw an FE go down, looking as if was out of control, with an HA diving on it. I dived on the HA and fired at it. I followed it down to about 2000 ft when I saw the FE flatten out, and I think it landed near Nouville Farm, but it passed beneath me. I then climbed up to 7000 ft and met another FE. We were both attacked by seven scouts. I climbed above the FE, and when the HA attacked it I dived on them. We fought for some minutes, and when I got to within 20 yards of a hostile scout I fired about 50 rounds at him. I saw tracers hit him, through the sight, and he stalled and spun. I last saw him spinning at about 3000 ft. The other HA dived away. Later, the FE attacked a scout below me, fighting with it for about five minutes. I saw tracers from the FE pass through its fuselage. It went into a nose dive and I lost sight of it. I think it was brought down.

'Five more FEs joined us and we were attacked by nine Albatros scouts. I climbed again above the FEs and dived on the HA, firing whenever I got my sight on one. A red Albatros scout with a larger engine than the rest dived on me from out of the sun. My gun jammed and I tried to break off the engagement, but the HA kept pace with me and opened fire, shooting away my pump and hitting the planes, so I then stopped and stunted. I then got under the HA and stopped there. I turned when it turned and dived when it dived. The HA pilot could not find me.

'I got my jam clear and fired on the HA, which was about 20 ft in front of me and about 10 ft above me. Half the fuselage and engine was all I could see through my sight. I saw tracers hit it. It started to climb, then stalled and went down in a dive, turning slowly. I last saw him at 1000 ft when I lost him in the mist. I saw two more scouts to the east of me and went to attack them but found I had no ammunition left. My machine was hit in three places during this combat.'

The prowess of Robert Little is certainly clear. He seldom hesitated to engage the enemy, even when in mechanical trouble, and he displayed the presence of mind to keep below an opponent, keeping one eye on him, while working to clear his jammed Vickers. And when this was done, rather than return home, he sought out more enemy fighters. Only when his ammunition was exhausted did Little break away.

The FE 2d 'pushers' mentioned in this engagement were from No 57 Squadron RFC, and they had been engaged over Douai by fighters from von Richthofen's JG Nr I, although the Baron was not flying that morning as he was preparing to go on leave. Von Richthofen had, however, scored four victories the day before to bring his personal score to 52. One of these had been Sopwith Triplane N5463, flown by Canadian Flt Sub-Lt A E Cuzner, who was killed.

The Baron's younger brother Lothar was leading *Jasta* 11 on the 30th, and he claimed one of the FEs, while another fell to the guns of *Jasta* 12's leader, Adolf von Tutschek. The dogfight had also seen 'Naval 8' claim five Albatros scouts 'out of control' – two to Little and one each to Compston, Booker and Flt Sub-Lt A R Knight.

For 2 May 1917 comes this from Little's log-book;

'1830 hrs, Triplane N5493, offensive patrol. At 1830 hrs I observed a formation of eight Albatros scouts attacking a formation of DH 4s. I dived on the nearest hostile scout when I was fired at from behind by another. I turned sharply and got under his tail, firing about 50 rounds at a range of about 10 to 15 yards. The HA came so near that I had to take my eyes off the sight to avoid colliding with it. The HA turned over on its side and then nose-dived. I was not able to watch it as my engine stopped at this moment. I glided west and was attacked by four hostile scouts. I dived towards our lines, and when over them spun down. I got my engine going again when at 300 ft. I climbed back up but the HA had gone. Lt Southern of No 25 Sqn RFC confirms that the HA I fired at went down out of control.'

For 9 May 1917, Little's log-book recorded;

0705 hrs, Triplane N5493, offensive patrol, Lens. Whilst on patrol at 0730 hrs in company with two other Triplanes, I observed two HA east of Lens, steering west. At the same time all the Triplanes attacked them, but we were then set upon by a large number of scouts from above. One Triplane had to break off the combat owing to a jammed gun, and the HA diving past me attacked Lt Wimbush, who was about 200 ft below me. He fought with them very well until his engine was shot and he himself was wounded. He escaped and made a forced landing near Koleuse les Mines. In the meantime I dived through the HA formation, firing about 100 rounds into one machine at a range of 50 yards. He dived straight down, but I was unable to ascertain his fate as I immediately attacked another machine.

'At 0810 hrs I was joined by another Triplane and some DH 4s, and the HA retired. As soon as the DH 4s had gone the HA returned. I was very much outnumbered, so I landed at St-Eloi to obtain reinforcements.

'At 0925 hrs, on report of enemy machines working west of Lens, I left St-Eloi in search. At 1010 hrs I observed two HA of the LVG type working at about 3000 ft west of Lens. I also saw two HA above them at about 10,000 ft. I dived on the nearest LVG and fired at it. The fight took us east of Lens and, after seeing tracers enter his centre section, he went down out of control south-east of Lens. I was then attacked by three two-seaters, and whilst manoeuvring with them I was attacked by a large number of scouts from above. As one passed me I fired and it spun under me. I am sure the pilot was hit, as he was so close to me. I then kept doing sharp turns, firing whenever I got my sight on a hostile machine. When I had run out of ammunition I broke off the combat by pushing my machine into a spin and then returned to St-Eloi.'

The Germans were still cock-a-hoop following their successes in 'Bloody April', and there were many combats for 'Naval 8' the following month. Indeed, the squadron claimed over 20 kills, and these mostly fell to Little, Booker, Simpson and Compston. For example, on the 18th (again flying N5493) Little had further reason to write a detailed report in his log-book following a mid-morning engagement;

'HA being observed from aerodrome, I left the ground in pursuit. I engaged the HA north-east of Lens at 10,000 ft at 1050 hrs and attacked from head-on. I then manoeuvred close in on him from astern. I fired about 100 rounds at the machine and the observer fired back at me. He fired about 20 rounds and then fell over the gun, and when the machine turned he fell back into the cockpit. I was so close to HA that I had to alter my course, do a half turn and then close in under his tail again. The observer was nowhere to be seen. I then fired again and the machine began to slip from side to side and go down. I followed it to 4000 ft and fired again at it. It then passed under my wing and I lost it in the mist. It was out of control (and AA battery reports seeing this machine go down out of control).

'I then observed a formation of HA and climbed to 13,000 ft to attack them. I attacked three two-seaters but was forced to break off the engagement as I was engaged by three Albatros scouts. After fighting with them for about ten minutes one went into a spin. I did not watch it as the other two were attacking me. They then retired east and I came home. A Nieuport squadron reports seeing one Albatros scout spin down and crash during the fight.'

These victories, and two more in late May, took Little's score to 20.

## OFFENSIVE PATROL

On 23 May 1917 Flt Lt R R Soar downed a two-seater LVG over La Bassée for his first victory in a Tri-

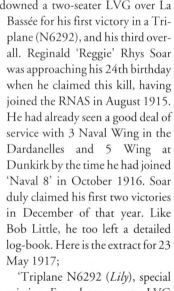

plane (N6292), and his third over-all. Reginald 'Reggie' Rhys Soar was approaching his 24th birthday when he claimed this kill, having joined the RNAS in August 1915. He had already seen a good deal of service with 3 Naval Wing in the Dardanelles and 5 Wing at Dunkirk by the time he had joined 'Naval 8' in October 1916. Soar duly claimed his first two victories in December of that year. Like Bob Little, he too left a detailed log-book. Here is the extract for 23 May 1917;

'Triplane N6292 (*Lily*), special mission. Found a two-seater LVG flying over La Bassée. Having out-climbed it, manoeuvring set in, so I attacked it. EA went east, but on my pretending to come home, it sat under the clouds, near Sainghin, where I dived on it and shot it down out of control. My victory was confirmed by Flt Lt Jenner-Parsons.

Immediately after the patrol, and soon after landing, I saw an enemy aircraft flying over our

**Three pilots of 8 Naval Squadron pose for the camera in early 1917. They are, from left to right, George Thom, H L Huskinson and future 12-kill ace R R Soar. Huskinson latter became the first CO of 4 Naval Squadron, leading the unit from its formation, on Pups, in March 1917 until July 1918, by which time it had become the RAF's No 204 Sqn** (*Franks collection*)

aerodrome at 3000 ft. Booker and I set off again and engaged him from over our aerodrome to Lens, where he was forced down. We subsequently landed in the dark. In the air for one hour.'

June opened with another emerging ace gaining his first confirmed success, Ronald Roscoe Thornely downing a two-seater in flames east of Lens on the morning of the 4th. Born in Cambridge in July 1889, Thornely and had seen action with the Royal Naval Armoured Car Squadron at Gallipoli before joining the RNAS in May 1916. He had been wounded in the chest on 9 September 1915 and was evacuated to a hospital ship in Alexandria harbour, where he came down with dysentery.

Returning to England, Thornely was taught to fly at Chingford, and before going to France he flew Home Defence patrols from Manston in early 1917. Arriving at 'Naval 8' in March 1917, he would gain three victories on Triplanes before the Camels arrived. By war's end Thornely had taken his score to ten, earning him the DSC. His first Triplane kill had been shared with Compston and Flt Sub-Lt E A Bennetts.

Thornely and Bennetts both scored victories on 7 June, and five days later another German machine was brought down by the squadron behind Allied lines. Several pilots were involved, and the kill was credited to Booker, Soar and Jenner-Parsons, with Thornely in attendance. Reggie Soar had forced another two-seater down shortly before this action. He wrote of the incident in his log-book;

'Triplane N6292 (*Lily*), OP, Douai–Epinoy–Cambrai. Many scraps. Whilst "Bookie" tackled an Aviatik I tackled his consort and shot him down in a slow spin near Ecourt St Quentin. Returning, we met five more Aviatik two-seaters being "Archied" near Gavrelle. Downed one. Landed in St Katherines near Arras. Pilot wounded in head, observer in stomach.'

These 'Naval 8' pilots seem a little underwhelmed about having their photograph taken following a dip in the St-Eloi swimming pool in the summer of 1917. They are, from left to right, Reggie Soar, H M Reid, J H D'Albiac DSO, J H Thompson, P A Johnston and E A Bennetts *(Sir Herbert Thompson via L A Rogers)*

Allied airmen often called all two-seaters 'Aviatiks', although few actually were. In this particular case, the downed two-seater was DFW C V serial number 9045/16 from the Bavarian Artillery *Flieger-abteilung* 288 (FA(A)288b), crewed by Ltns Franz Nieberle and Johannes von Pieverling. Reggie Soar obviously had access to the captured two-seater, or to a subsequent report about it, for he noted in the back of his log-book;

'DFW Aviatik shot down. Booker, James (Jenner-Parsons) and self, 12 June 1917. Two-seater. Military No 9045/16, engine 220 hp Benz No 30285, propeller ETA type disc 3000, pitch 1.900 (metres), tyres 8.0 x 125 Continental, ammunition – armour piercing, armour piercing tracer and a few explosive tracer. In the pilot's cockpit is a socket for an electric plug with an aluminium notice plate fixed by it to the effect that it is for a heating circuit, probably for electrically-heated clothing. The machine was fitted with a wireless and had two sending keys, but it is not known whether both keys were for the observer or one for the observer and one for the pilot. There is a fan-driven wireless generator giving, as usual, both direct and alternating current, the former being used to excite the alternator. The total output of the direct current side is, however, four amps at 50 volts, which is at least three times as is required for the exciter current, and the balance is probably used for the heating circuit.'

Two more two-seaters were destroyed on 16 June, with one again falling behind British lines. Little and Flt Sub-Lt P A Johnston got one at 0930 hrs, while Compston and Thornely had bagged theirs behind the frontline an hour earlier. The latter was another DFW C V (5046/17), which came down at Liévin, near Lens. It had a large number '6' on its fuselage, and was crewed by Ltns Niebecker and Friedrich Karl Riegel of FA(A)211 – Niebecker was wounded, and Riegel was sent to Holyport Prison Camp (as No 1143). The C V was allocated the RFC serial G 47.

Little went on to score two confirmed victories on 21 and 26 June, as recorded in his log-book, while he and Reggie Soar claimed an Albatros shared on the 29th. Of the 21 June action he wrote;

'Triplane N5493, 0920 hrs, offensive patrol. While on OP over the lines, we met four Albatros scouts over Courriers at 1030 hrs at 12,000 ft. Flt Lt Johnston climbed above them and I dived below them. The HA then made circuits, trying to climb up to Flt Lt Johnston. One HA dropped behind the rest and I attacked it at once, firing at very close range. He went down into a flat spin. I dived after him and fired at him all the way down to the clouds, at 7000 ft. I went through them to 4000 ft and saw him crash about a mile east of the white line near Henin-Lietard.'

Five days later, Little recorded;

'26 June 1917, Triplane N5493, 1740 hrs, special mission. On seeing HA from the aerodrome, I was sent up to engage it. I met HA east of St-Eloi and attacked it head-on from a little below. I then did a roll, which brought me out about 20 yards behind, going in the same direction as HA. I then stalled up and fired a burst of 20 rounds at a range of 50 yards. The HA stalled and dived west. I went after the HA, which dived past the vertical and came back east on its back. Something then fell out – I think it was a man. The machine glided on its back and I caught up to it again. I saw a man crawling along the fuselage, trying to get on the bottom (the machine was still on its back and was now on fire). I closed in on the HA and fired about 20 rounds at it and the man fell off. The machine carried on down to about 180 ft, where it broke up and crashed near Acheville.'

The luckless crew would appear to have been Gftr Ernst Bittorf and Ltn Karl Schweizer of FA269(A), who came down between Fresnoy and Drocourt, south-east of Lens. A report from an ground-based observer stated;

'One Sopwith Triplane engaged an enemy machine over the line Vimy-Oppy. The enemy came to ground about one mile behind Acheville, out of control. One man fell from machine while fighting. The Triplane had the advantage all through the fight.'

Bob Little's 16 June kill had been shared with fellow Australian Philip Andrew Johnston, who enjoyed further success on 21 June. Born in Sydney in February 1898, he performed Home Defence duties in 1916 before joining 8 Naval Squadron in France during 'Bloody April'. Johnston claimed three Triplane victories in May and June, and would become an ace when the squadron re-equipped with Camels. His brief combat career came to an abrupt halt on 17 August 1917 when he was killed in a mid-air collision with B A Bennetts over Wingles. German pilots were never reluctant to claim victories, and in this instance Hans Bethge, *Staffelführer* of *Jasta* 30, was credited with his 12th and 13th kills.

On 29 June 1917 Little wrote in his log-book;

'Triplane N5493, 1700 hrs, special mission. I observed seven EA over Lens. I also saw "C" Flight coming towards me, so I waited until Flt Lt Soar came up and then dived at the rearmost machine and opened fire on it. I saw tracer hit this HA, which turned to the left, and Soar then began to fire at it. We were both firing at it when it went down.'

Soar described the incident as follows;

'Triplane N6292, special mission. To drive off seven Albatroses reported on lines. 1700 hrs, on Aviatik, but he was too quick for me. Little and I attacked the seven scouts and engaged and concentrated on one, which we shot down. This was reported from trenches to crash in houses of Saloumines.'

As July opened, Little and Soar were again scoring, both claiming an Albatros on the 3rd and sharing another on the 5th. Soar described these combats in his log-book;

'3 July 1917, Triplane N6292, OP, Douai. After keeping two flocks of scouts east of Douai, I attacked and drove down one our of control, and so did Jenner-Parsons, who confirmed mine. Later, I had a 15-minute scrap with a clever one.

'5 July 1917, Triplane N6292, special mission, Pont-à-Vendin –Wingles. After a lengthy fight with a two-seater Aviatik at Pont-à-Vendin, I got a good burst in at close range and he went down out of control, disappearing through clouds still out of control.'

Soar made further interesting log-book entries a few days later which offer observations on life with a World War 1 fighting squadron;

'10 July, Triplane N6292, OP, Tampoux–Izel les Esquerchin. Little and self engaged four flocks of EA of six each. Little shot one down and I kept the others off him with McCudden.

'11 July, Triplane N6292, special mission – Drocourt Line. Aviatik two-seater attempting to take photos this side of lines at about 12,000 ft, with me under his engine. I prevented this (*text continues on page 46*)

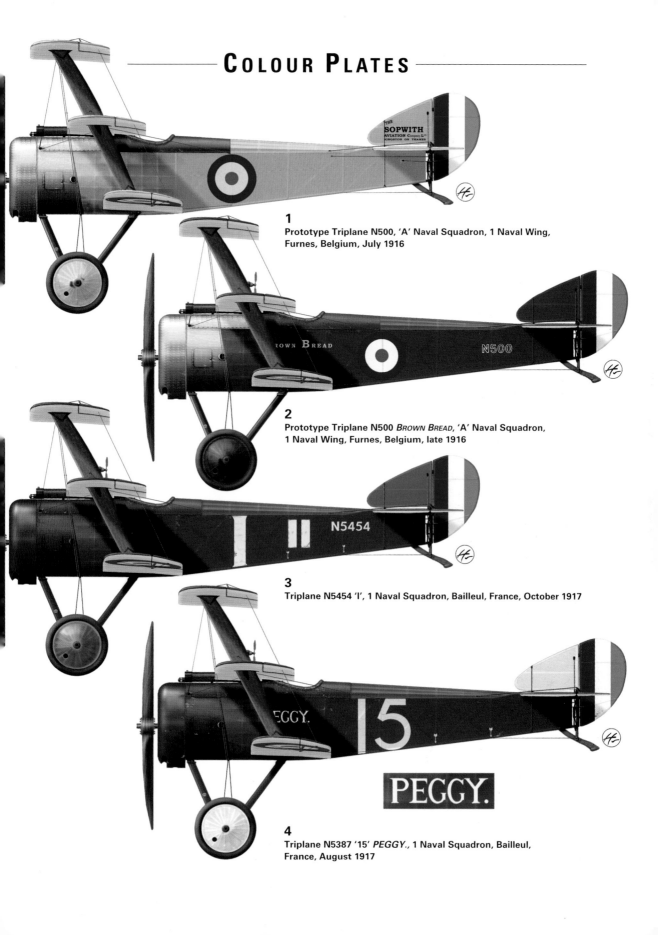

# COLOUR PLATES

**1**
Prototype Triplane N500, 'A' Naval Squadron, 1 Naval Wing,
Furnes, Belgium, July 1916

**2**
Prototype Triplane N500 *BROWN BREAD*, 'A' Naval Squadron,
1 Naval Wing, Furnes, Belgium, late 1916

**3**
Triplane N5454 'I', 1 Naval Squadron, Bailleul, France, October 1917

**4**
Triplane N5387 '15' *PEGGY.*, 1 Naval Squadron, Bailleul,
France, August 1917

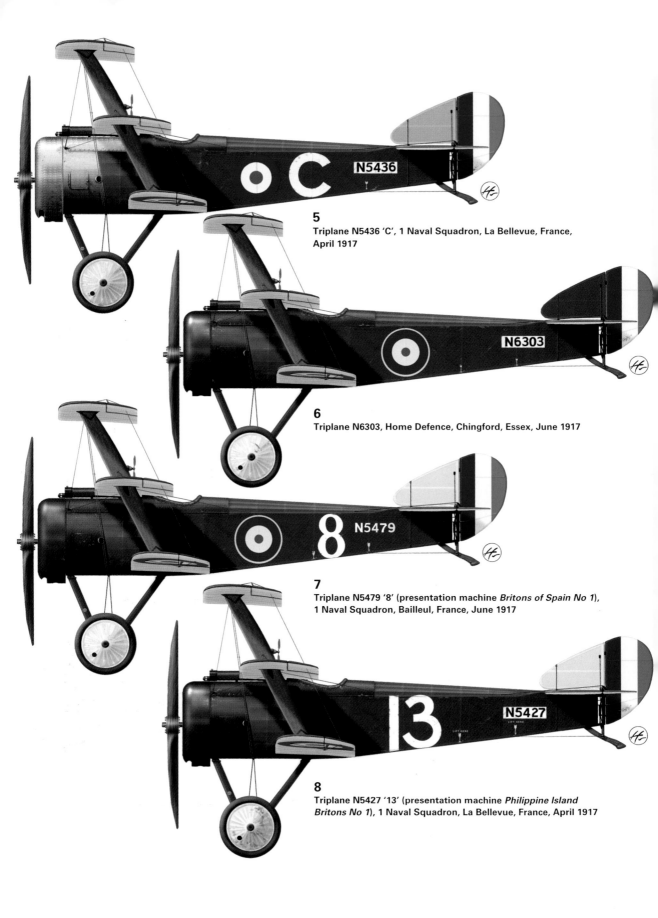

**5**
Triplane N5436 'C', 1 Naval Squadron, La Bellevue, France,
April 1917

**6**
Triplane N6303, Home Defence, Chingford, Essex, June 1917

**7**
Triplane N5479 '8' (presentation machine *Britons of Spain No 1*),
1 Naval Squadron, Bailleul, France, June 1917

**8**
Triplane N5427 '13' (presentation machine *Philippine Island
Britons No 1*), 1 Naval Squadron, La Bellevue, France, April 1917

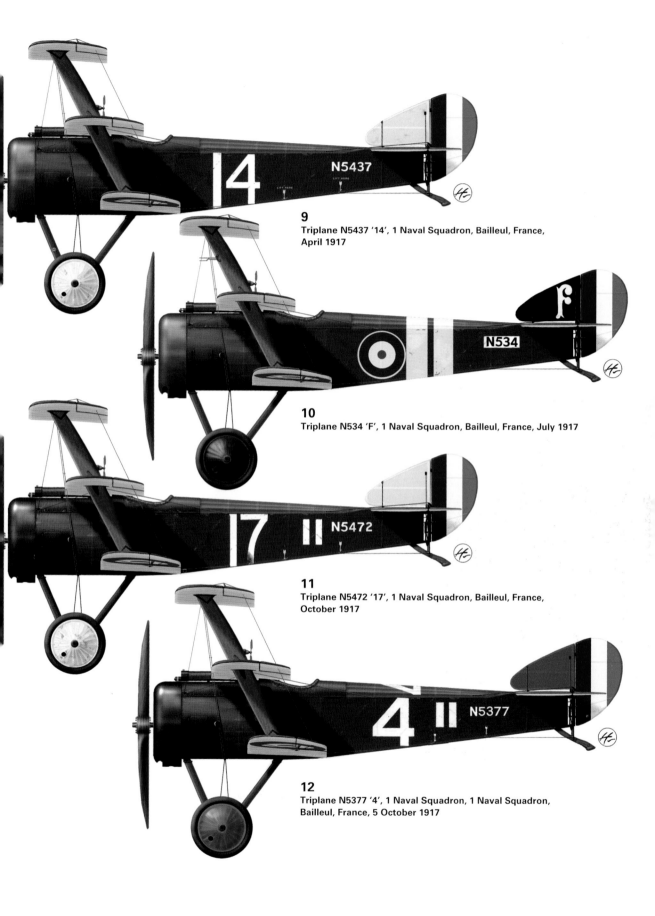

**9**
Triplane N5437 '14', 1 Naval Squadron, Bailleul, France,
April 1917

**10**
Triplane N534 'F', 1 Naval Squadron, Bailleul, France, July 1917

**11**
Triplane N5472 '17', 1 Naval Squadron, Bailleul, France,
October 1917

**12**
Triplane N5377 '4', 1 Naval Squadron, 1 Naval Squadron,
Bailleul, France, 5 October 1917

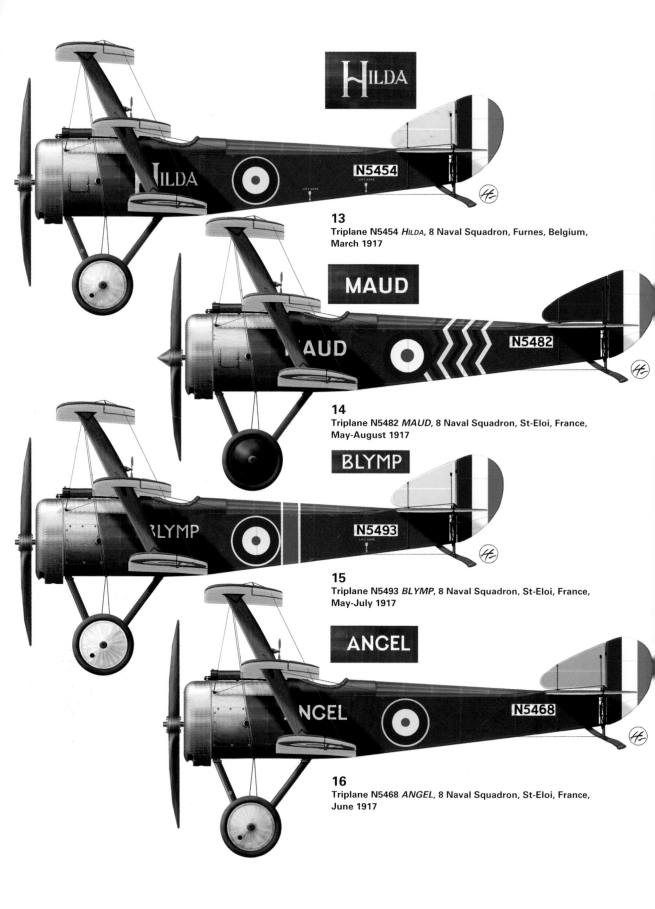

**HILDA**

**13**
Triplane N5454 *HILDA*, 8 Naval Squadron, Furnes, Belgium,
March 1917

**MAUD**

**14**
Triplane N5482 *MAUD*, 8 Naval Squadron, St-Eloi, France,
May-August 1917

**BLYMP**

**15**
Triplane N5493 *BLYMP*, 8 Naval Squadron, St-Eloi, France,
May-July 1917

**ANGEL**

**16**
Triplane N5468 *ANGEL,* 8 Naval Squadron, St-Eloi, France,
June 1917

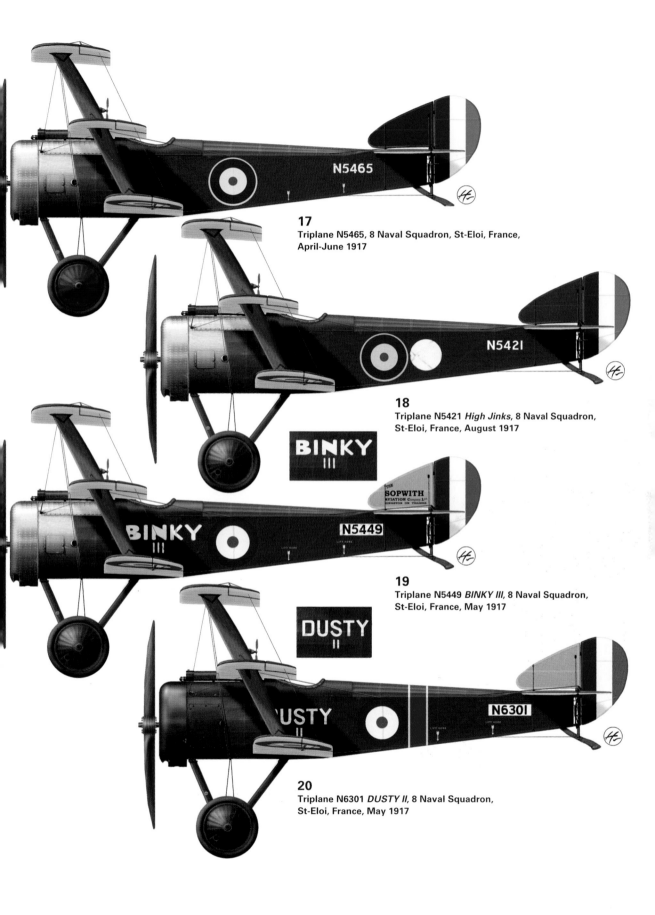

**17**
Triplane N5465, 8 Naval Squadron, St-Eloi, France,
April-June 1917

**18**
Triplane N5421 *High Jinks*, 8 Naval Squadron,
St-Eloi, France, August 1917

**19**
Triplane N5449 *BINKY III*, 8 Naval Squadron,
St-Eloi, France, May 1917

**20**
Triplane N6301 *DUSTY II*, 8 Naval Squadron,
St-Eloi, France, May 1917

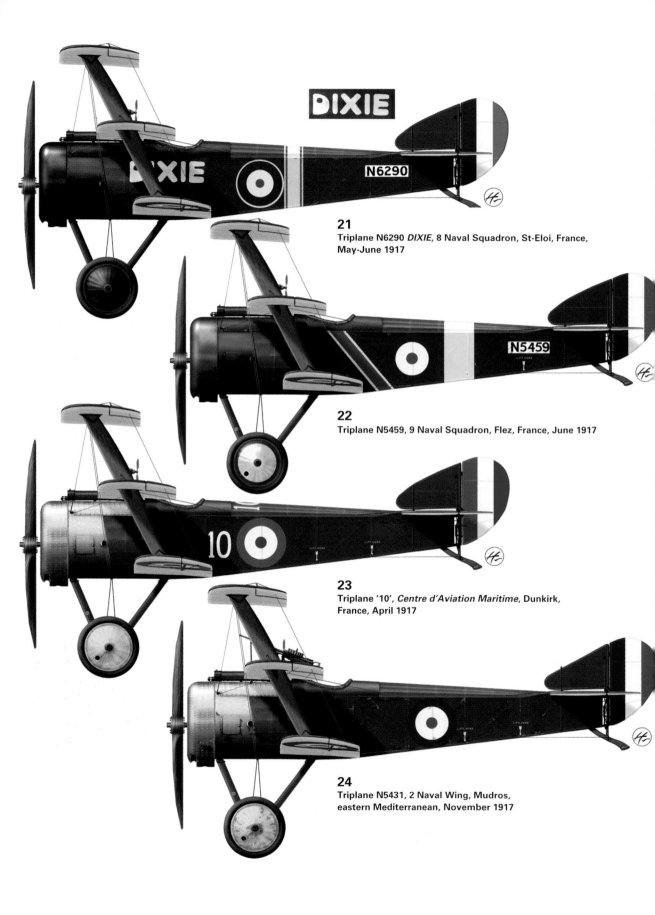

**21**
Triplane N6290 *DIXIE*, 8 Naval Squadron, St-Eloi, France,
May-June 1917

**22**
Triplane N5459, 9 Naval Squadron, Flez, France, June 1917

**23**
Triplane '10', *Centre d'Aviation Maritime*, Dunkirk,
France, April 1917

**24**
Triplane N5431, 2 Naval Wing, Mudros,
eastern Mediterranean, November 1917

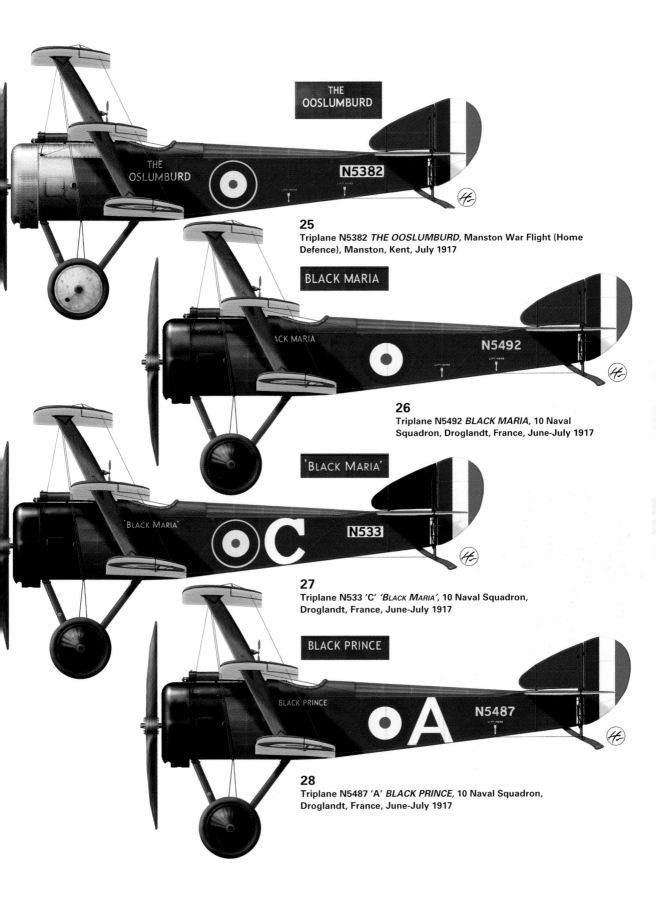

**THE OOSLUMBURD**

**25**
Triplane N5382 *THE OOSLUMBURD*, Manston War Flight (Home Defence), Manston, Kent, July 1917

**BLACK MARIA**

**26**
Triplane N5492 *BLACK MARIA*, 10 Naval Squadron, Droglandt, France, June-July 1917

**'BLACK MARIA'**

**27**
Triplane N533 'C' *'BLACK MARIA'*, 10 Naval Squadron, Droglandt, France, June-July 1917

**BLACK PRINCE**

**28**
Triplane N5487 'A' *BLACK PRINCE,* 10 Naval Squadron, Droglandt, France, June-July 1917

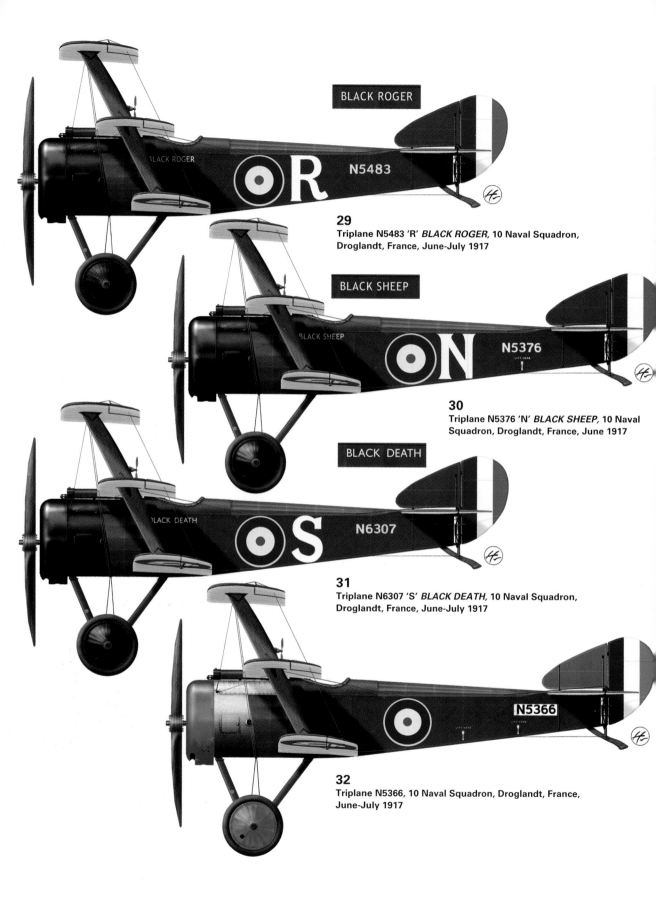

**BLACK ROGER**

**29**
Triplane N5483 'R' *BLACK ROGER,* 10 Naval Squadron,
Droglandt, France, June-July 1917

**BLACK SHEEP**

**30**
Triplane N5376 'N' *BLACK SHEEP,* 10 Naval
Squadron, Droglandt, France, June 1917

**BLACK DEATH**

**31**
Triplane N6307 'S' *BLACK DEATH,* 10 Naval Squadron,
Droglandt, France, June-July 1917

**32**
Triplane N5366, 10 Naval Squadron, Droglandt, France,
June-July 1917

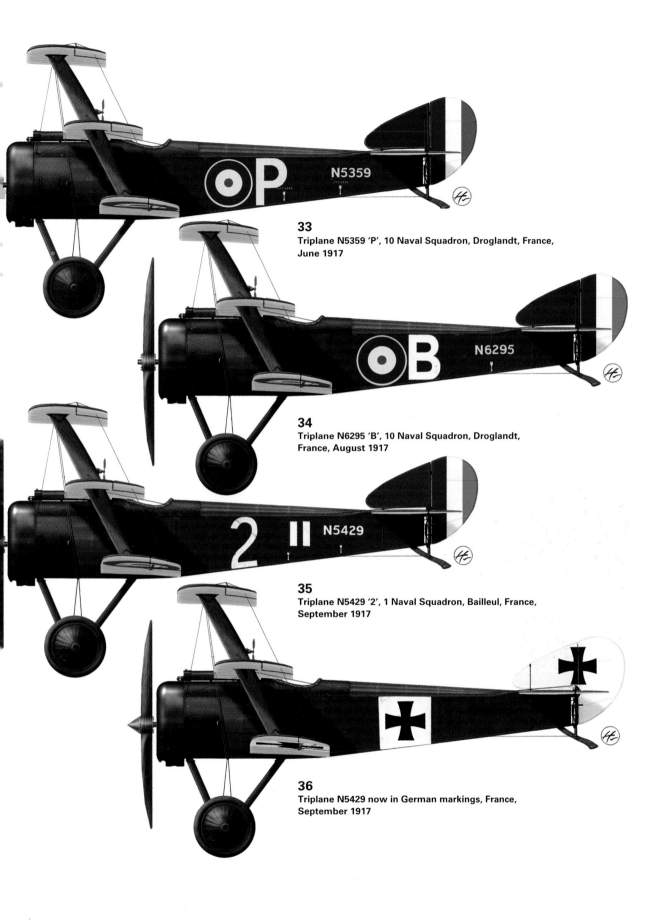

**33**
Triplane N5359 'P', 10 Naval Squadron, Droglandt, France,
June 1917

**34**
Triplane N6295 'B', 10 Naval Squadron, Droglandt,
France, August 1917

**35**
Triplane N5429 '2', 1 Naval Squadron, Bailleul, France,
September 1917

**36**
Triplane N5429 now in German markings, France,
September 1917

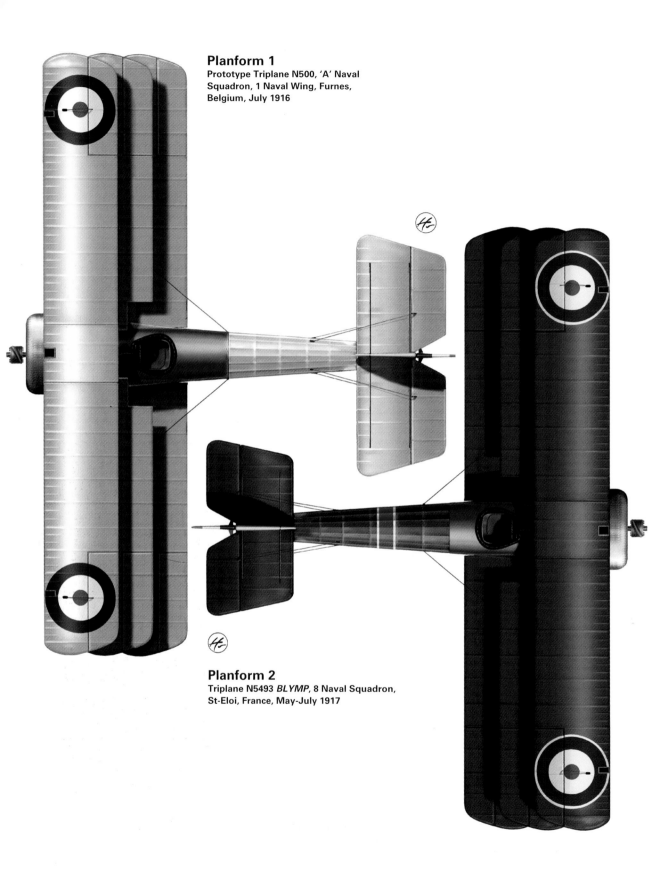

**Planform 1**
Prototype Triplane N500, 'A' Naval
Squadron, 1 Naval Wing, Furnes,
Belgium, July 1916

**Planform 2**
Triplane N5493 *BLYMP*, 8 Naval Squadron,
St-Eloi, France, May-July 1917

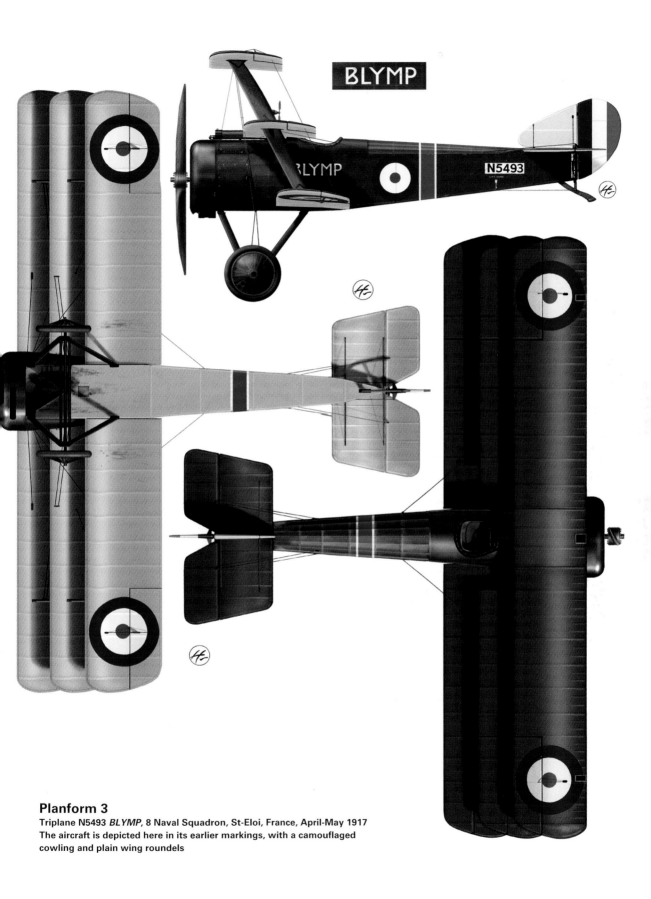

**Planform 3**
Triplane N5493 *BLYMP*, 8 Naval Squadron, St-Eloi, France, April-May 1917
The aircraft is depicted here in its earlier markings, with a camouflaged
cowling and plain wing roundels

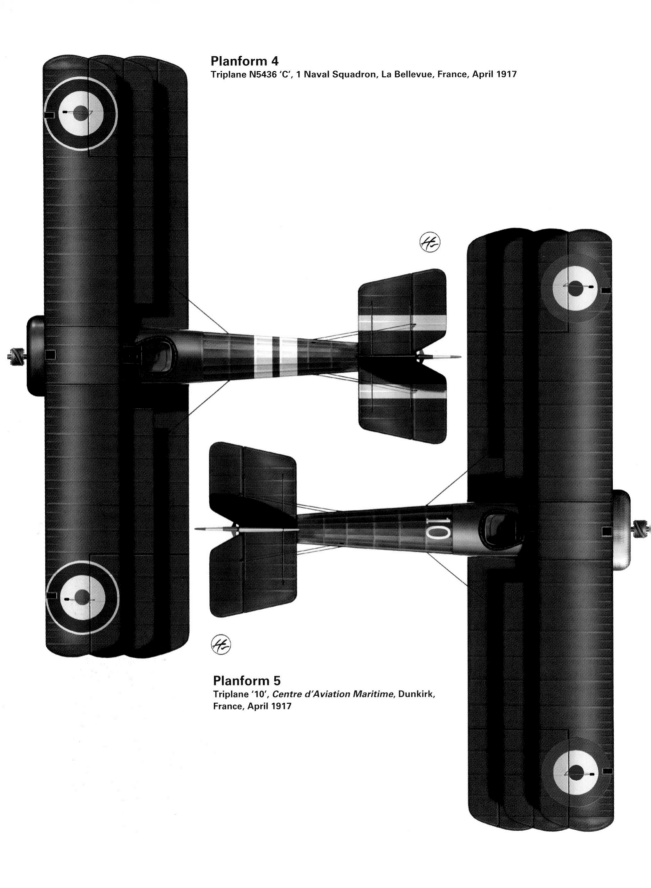

**Planform 4**
Triplane N5436 'C', 1 Naval Squadron, La Bellevue, France, April 1917

**Planform 5**
Triplane '10', *Centre d'Aviation Maritime*, Dunkirk,
France, April 1917

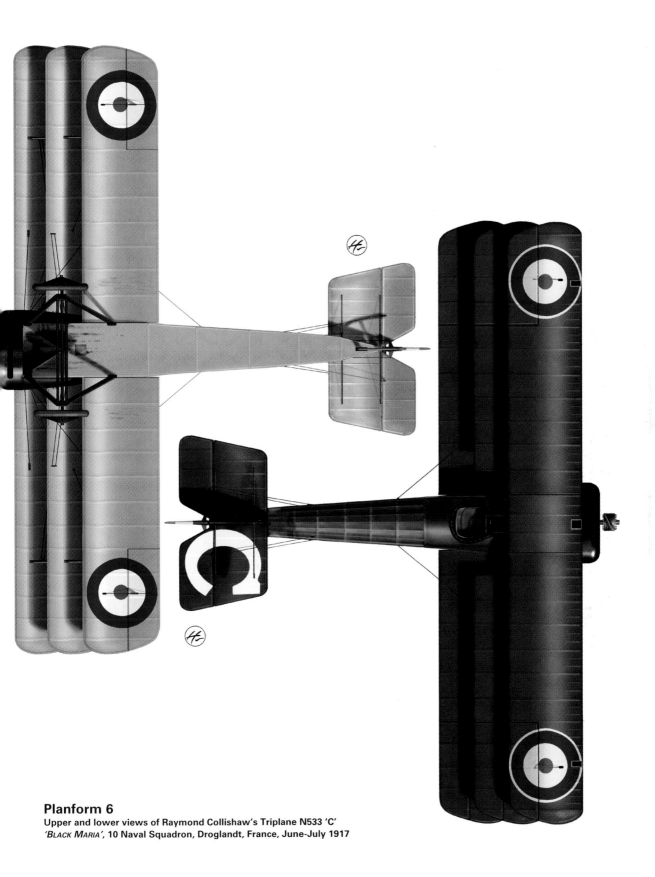

**Planform 6**
Upper and lower views of Raymond Collishaw's Triplane N533 'C'
*'BLACK MARIA'*, 10 Naval Squadron, Droglandt, France, June-July 1917

by continually stalling and firing, and when I got him to turn home, I think I killed his observer. Saw a tracer hit empennage and come out of his top wing. Thompson and self.

'13 July, Triplane N6292, OP. Booker, Thompson and self drove down three Albatros at Henin Lietard and three others lost from Avion. Also got two spotters from Izel les Esquerchin. Nothing certain.'

On a later patrol on the 13th, Little and Soar, both flying Sopwith Camels, shot down a DFW two-seater between Lens and Pelves. This proved to be a busy day, as both pilots flew missions. Although Little now flew the first of the new Camels, Reggie Soar continued to stick mostly with his faithful Triplanes after this one day on the new type.

With the arrival of brand new Camels at St-Eloi, pilots used both Sopwith types for a while. In the famous book *Naval Eight*, edited by E G Johnstone (who was himself a Camel ace with 8 Naval Squadron/ No 208 Sqn RAF) and first published in 1931, Geoffrey Bromet wrote;

'Early in July we started to change our Triplanes for Sopwith Camels, and the note in the Squadron Diary for the 10 July that Arnold, Johnston and Knight flew *Dixie, Veda* and *Peter III* to Dunkirk will recall some of the names we had for machines in those days. "The Frivolities" entertained the ship's company that night. We were still very naval, you see.'

Some of 8 Naval Squadron's Triplanes featured a variety of names painted on the aircraft, including *Dixie*/N6290, flown by Rex Arnold, Reggie Soar's *Lily*/N6292, Jenner-Parsons' *ANGEL*/N5468, McDonald's *DUSTY II*/N6301 and Bob Little's *BLYMP*/N5493. Soar also flew *HILDA*/N5454 (named after a cousin) and other names included *Snapp*, *Pip*/N5442, *Gwen*/N5474, *Joan*/N5449, *Willa*/N5455, Booker's *MAUD*/N5482, G G Simpson's *BINKY III*/N5449and *Peggy*/N5425.

Bob Little scored his last Triplane victory on 10 July and gained his first on a Camel 48 hours later. As mentioned above, he and Reggie Soar, also

Triplane N5468, pictured at Furnes, in Belgium, was flown by C H B Jenner-Parsons in early 1917 *(T Mellor-Ellis collection)*

By March 1917 Jenner-Parsons' 'C' Flight aircraft N5468 had been named *ANGEL*. The Triplane parked next to it in this photograph is N5465, which was used by R R Thornely to gain five kills, E D Crundell one kill and 'Naval 1's' S M Kinkead six kills *(via Andy Thomas)*

Reggie Soar's N5454 *HILDA* saw most of its action after leaving 'Naval 8' for 'Naval 1', where it became R P Minifie's white '1'. He used it to claim 10 of his 17 Triplane kills

in a Camel, shot down an Aviatik (actually another DFW C type) on the 13th, although the latter ace then returned to his favourite Triplane, N6292. Two days later, and again on the 17th, Soar and Booker each claimed an Albatros .

Reggie Soar once wrote of Little;

'On the Somme front he was immediately successful in fights in the air, as he was with tricks on the ground. For instance, the pilots would often take a tender into Amiens for dinner at the Godbert. Very often we would get stuck behind a car full of French officers en route, who would not give way to the "vile Anglaise", so Little would pull out his revolver and shoot a nice round hole in the rear tyre of their tourer. He never missed! He was

an outstanding shot with both revolver and rifle, and was also a collector of wild flowers. He had few equals when it came to air fighting, and although not a polished pilot, he was one of the most aggressive. He would fly the whole length of the British front, from the floods at Nieuport to St Quentin if there was nothing to fight on "Naval 8"s own Lens-Arras front.'

In later life Bob Little's widow recorded;

'Alex was of average height, and although it is so many years since I last saw him, I still remember very well what he looked like. He was well proportioned, with hazel eyes which appeared forever alert. His movements, too, were quick and decisive and were made without waste of energy. He also had a sense of humour which his photographs belie.'

In *Naval Eight,* R J O Compston says of his friend Bob Little;

'He was not so much a leader as a brilliant lone hand. I feel safe in saying that there have been few better shots, either in the services or outside, than this man. I have seen him bring down a crow on the wing with a .22-cal rifle, and break bottles thrown into the air while they were still travelling upwards. What more deadly foe could be found than such a man, armed with two machine guns firing at the rate of 2000 rounds per minute? Once Little came within range of an enemy he did not give up until, first, the enemy was shot down, secondly, his own engine failed, or thirdly, he ran out of ammunition. He had in human guise the fighting tendencies of a bulldog. He never let go.

'Small in stature, with face set grimly, he seemed the epitome of deadliness. Sitting aloft with the eyes of a hawk, he dealt death with unfailing precision. Seldom did he return to the aerodrome reporting an indecisive combat, for as long as petrol and ammunition held out, Little held on until the enemy's machine either broke up or burst into flames.'

Compston himself wrote of his own experiences in *Naval Eight*;

'I remember one of my own pilots, seeing me fire at something (he did not see it was an enemy aeroplane, although we were very close to it), fired his guns – presumably in sympathy – hitting the middle plane of my Triplane about 12 inches from my right shoulder. The following incident also illustrates what I have said about "air sight". I was asked by one of the pilots in the squadron if I would lead him to a position where he could see a real live enemy. He had done a number of patrols, but had not been in close contact with the enemy.

'We set out together, and after gaining a good height (17,000 ft) I was fortunate enough to see an enemy two-seater coming from our own side of the lines. I say fortunate, because these aircraft were very difficult to engage, being capable of attaining great height, and they were fast. In fact, in some instances I have known such machines to have been faster and better climbers that out own fighting scouts of the time.

'Although the enemy machine was about 1000 ft above us when I first saw it, we managed by a series of dives and climbs to arrive in a suitable position underneath and, pulling up vertically, I put a stream of bullets through which the pilot had to fly. Having lost all speed in the vertical climb, I fell over onto my back, but while falling I saw the enemy machine make a flat turn (without banking) and nearly hit my pilot. Steeper and steeper dived the stricken enemy, until his port wings came off and he crashed near Loos, where we collected the wreckage later.

**Although of poor quality, this rare photograph shows Bob Little's N5493 *BLYMP*, which he used to score 20 of his 24 Triplane victories (*via P Jarrett*)**

'On arrival at our aerodrome the pilot told me that he saw nothing at all, except the machine which nearly hit him. He neither saw it come nor did he know to what end it had dived past him. Incidentally, neither the pilot nor the observer of the German machine could have known what was happening, for the pilot was shot in the head and the observer in the heart.'

Soar's log-book for 17 July 1917 contains this entry;

'Triplane N6292, OP, near Douai aerodrome. After driving off some Albatri, Booker and self dived and took unawares two others near Douai aerodrome. Got one (confirmed).'

Charles Booker got a Rumpler two-seater on the 20th, and this seems to have been 8 Naval Squadron's last Triplane victory – Camels replaced all of them between late July and early August. Reggie Soar certainly continued to fly his till late July, and even Little's N5493 *BLYMP* on the 22nd, driving seven two-seaters away from the lines. Two days later came the announcement that Soar had been awarded the DSC.

He subsequently wrote about his flight in Bob Little's machine;

'I flew his Triplane *BLYMP* when he was on leave and mine was on overhaul. I found I was overshooting (during attacks) until I look at the speed. I saw I was coming in at 80 instead of 50/60 knots. I later found out that Little had his seat moved forward a bit so that he could dive faster, the crazy clown!'

On 5 August Soar noted in his log-book that he had taken *Lily*/N6292 up to Dunkirk, landing at Petite Synthe, to change it for another machine. It is interesting that he returned not with a new Camel, but another Triplane, N5421 *High Jinks*. This Triplane had been with the squadron earlier in the year but had been damaged in a landing accident. Now repaired, it was back. In his log-book Soar put it this way;

**E D Crundell DSC scored three Triplane victories with 8 Naval Squadron and four more on Camels with the RAF's No 210 Sqn** *(Franks collection)*

'To Dunkerque. Landed first at Petit Synthe. Changing *Lily* for another bus. From Dunkerque to St-Eloi. This is old *High Jinks* (Simpson's bus) patched up.'

It was strange that Soar should note the aircraft as fellow ace G G Simpson's old machine, for although he may have flown it on occasion, he did not achieve any combat successes with it. But Soar flew this Triplane throughout the first half of August, which was to represent his last days with 'Naval 8'. It is obvious, too, from his log-book that the squadron was operating mixed patrols of Triplanes and Camels;

'11 August 1917, Triplane N5421, OP Quiry la Motte–Pont á Vendin. Lots of EA. "Bookie" got one smoking as he shot at it going down but he was shot down and landed safely at Farbus. Camels, three Triplanes, eight Bristol Fighters, six Nieuports and six SE 5s formed up later. Albatros scouts came up and several engagements took place. Five Albatros driven down.

'13 August, N5421. Kept spotting machines away from Drocourt Line. Uneventful.

'14 August, N5421, OP. Drove three flocks of Albatros down. Heavy AA. End of Arras Campaign. Discharged from active service to Cranwell. Time on active service, 322.5 hours, as far as I can prove.'

Several future aces also opened their scores while flying the Triplane, including Roderick McDonald from Nova Scotia. Born in October 1893, he had joined the RNAS in August 1916 after learning to fly at the Curtiss School, and by the following spring he was with 'Naval 8'. McDonald scored three kills in May, then went on to achieve a further five with the Camel and become a flight commander. However, on 8 May 1918 he was shot down and killed by Vfw Julius Trotsky of *Jasta* 43.

'Naval 8' had achieved many successes during the late spring and early summer of 1917. Around 70 victories had been claimed and two DSOs (Bromet and Little), five DSCs (Huskinson, Compston, Booker, Simpson and Soar), two Bars to DSCs (Little and Compston) and a CdG (Little) awarded.

The author was fortunate enough to meet ace Edward Crundell many years ago. Born in Whitfield, Dover, in December 1896, he had joined the RNAS in July 1916 and been posted to the fighter unit in February 1917. Although Crundell only scored a modest three Triplane victories with 'Naval 8', he did go on to secure seven kill in all flying Camels with No 210 Sqn in 1918, for which he was awarded the DFC. When he arrived in the frontline, 8 Naval Squadron had just two Triplanes and one Nieuport two-seater on strength, so he flew with 'Naval 9' until his unit attained sufficient aircraft to be declared operational

One of those machines sent to the unit was the second Triplane prototype, N504, which had eventually reached the front in December 1916. Pilots flew it for 'experience on type' firstly with 'Naval 1', then 'Naval 9' and finally 'Naval 8'. Reggie Soar suffered engine trouble while flying this aircraft on 26 February 1917, and had to force land it in a ploughed field. Ed Crundell noted in his diary, which formed the basis for his book *Fighter Pilot on the Western Front*;

'During the morning Soar took up Sopwith Triplane No 9. This machine was rather tricky on the engine control, and he choked the engine when gliding in, so he could not quite reach the aerodrome. He came down in a ploughed field and the Triplane turned on to its nose, breaking the propeller and inflicting damage on the leading edge of the top plane.'

The Triplane obviously took a bit of getting used to, according to Crundell's diary entry for the 28th;

'Jenner-Parsons and Allen flew a Triplane for the first time. Jenner landed too fast and Allen too slowly. Millward was the next to fly the Triplane, but he came in too high and nearly ran into a ditch. Knight did quite well. I was the last to fly it. When getting off the ground the propeller tip struck a mole hill, breaking off the trailing edge. At the time I did not realise anything out of the ordinary had happened, but in the air the machine vibrated badly. I climbed at a good steep angle and circled around for 15 minutes and then made a good landing. The aileron controls were very sensitive.'

On 17 March Crundell had a close call, inexperience being the main cause;

'I went on an early morning patrol with Soar over the Nieuport floods. Apparently a Hun passed over us about 1000 ft away, which I had thought was a British machine. Soar said it got on my tail and fired at me. I had heard a noise, which I assumed was the flapping of wires on my Triplane. He blamed me for not taking proper precautions, and said if I continued to act in that way I should not be alive much longer. A few bullet holes were found in my machine.'

But he had a better day on 14 April, gaining his first two victories;

'At 0800 hrs Booker led "C" Flight on a patrol to escort the FEs of No 25 Sqn RFC who were on photographic duty. My engine was running badly and I could not keep up with the formation. At about 0900 hrs, when a long way over the German side of the lines, I saw two machines flying parallel to the west. I had never seen a type of aeroplane quite like them. They looked somewhat like Nieuports, but much bigger. I realised they were probably Huns which "C" Flight had not seen. I was a bit scared because I was a straggler all on my own, and those ominous-looking aeroplanes blocked my way to safety. I was at a great disadvantage because my engine was running so badly.

'I realised I must make a decision. The thought of being taken prisoner terrified me, so I decided to go and have a look and sell my life as dearly as possible if I had to fight. I climbed as steeply as I could and they im-mediately did likewise, so I became more suspicious than ever. They were about two or three miles away, so when slightly above them I turned abruptly to the left and approached. At about 100 yards distance I saw they were both two-seaters, and almost immediately afterwards I spied an Iron Cross (marking) on the top plane of one of them, so I knew for certain they were Huns.

'At that instant one of the observers in the back seat opened fire on me. This made me furious. I literally saw red and dived on the tail of the nearest, firing my gun all the time. I got closer and closer to his tail until I was almost touching it and I could see the heads of the pilot and observer heads and every detail of the machine. Suddenly the German machine fell over on one wing and went down in a steep dive. I was thrilled and started to relax, but only for a moment because I was attacked from behind by the other machine. Again I saw red and was just as furious as on the first occasion. I swung round, got on his tail and fired at the same close range.

**Although not an ace, Flt Cdr C H B Jenner-Parsons still enjoyed some success at the controls of a 'Naval 8' Triplane in 1917**

**R B Munday DSC scored his first victory with 8 Naval Squadron while flying a Triplane, and duly went on to score eight more with Camels (*T Mellor-Ellis collection*)**

'After a long spell of firing he started to dive, and it got steeper and steeper until I realised the Triplane's wings would break off if I increased my own dive. Previously, I had thrown caution to the winds because, as I entered each flight, I did not expect to come out of them alive. So I shut off the engine and eased the Triplane out of the dive when I found it very left wing heavy, and I had to fly with the stick fully over to the right. I had started the first fight at 14,000 ft in the vicinity of Lens and ended the second at 7000 ft to the east of Douai. The engine had been running at full throttle all the time.

'I was very heavily "archied" on the return journey to the lines and, owing to a strong westerly wind, it took me about 30 minutes to regain them, being fairly plastered with "archie" and "flaming onions" all the time. After crossing the lines I did not recognise any landmarks so, when I spotted an aerodrome, I landed. I got the machine filled with petrol and oil and set off for Auchel.

'On arrival at Auchel I was told to report to Sqn Cdr Bromet, who questioned me about the fights and told me to write my combat reports. He thinks the enemy machines were Albatros two-seaters. When I returned to "C" Flight I was told my Triplane was almost falling to pieces, and quite unsafe to fly in its present condition. The flying wires were stretched and very slack, and one of the centre section struts had cracked and bent out of shape. Only one bullet hole had been found, which was in the lowest left-hand plane. After I had left the formation to attack the two Albatros two-seaters, Booker attacked and shot down a German LVG two-seater biplane, which was seen to crash. Soar attacked three other Huns but he could not get close enough to do any real damage.

'Early in the afternoon Sqn Cdr Bromet called me again and said he was convinced I had shot down both enemy aircraft. They were seen to crash by independent witnesses. An observer in a kite balloon saw the first one dive into the ground and explode. The other was seen to hit the ground and burst into flames by Capt Leith, the flight commander of No 25 Sqn RFC whose FEs we were escorting. At the time he was flying at 4000 ft taking photographs.'

Crundell had been flying N5464 *Doris* on this occasion, and he gained victory number three on 18 August in N5465. In the meantime, he had himself been brought down – by AA fire – again flying *Doris* on 10 May. The squadron had just begun its move to St-Eloi, and Crundell had set off alone at 0915 hrs to look for enemy aircraft along the front. He met considerable AA fire, as he recorded;

'Then I saw a two-seater Aviatik above me, so I climbed to 9000 ft and got under it, and it was climbing almost as fast as I was. I pulled my Triplane up into a stalling position and fired a burst at the German, but lost 1000 ft of my height in the stall and the Aviatik climbed out of range. Then the anti-aircraft guns really let me have it, one burst hitting my Triplane. I felt a violent stab in the back, as though someone had struck me a heavy blow with a hammer, and the engine stopped. Petrol was pouring in gallons over my boots and ceased to flow in less than half a minute. I was then about six miles on the German side of the lines at a height of 8000 ft.

'I glided towards the lines through a terrific bombardment and crossed them at 3000 ft. After I had crossed the trenches the bombardment

ceased, and I felt very faint. I could feel blood running down my back. I put my head out into the wind to revive myself and set the tail trim to the slow glide position in case I did faint. I steered towards Béthune because I assumed it would have a hospital.'

Ed Crundell got down safely and later found himself in a casualty clearing station. A piece of shrapnel had missed his spine by a fraction of an inch. The AA shell had badly damaged his Triplane, with a large hole being punched in the petrol tank. It must have been almost a direct hit, so he was lucky to have survived. He did not return to his unit until July.

Crundell confided an interesting observation to his diary about the Triplane's ammunition belts. He said that *Doris* had been fitted with new metal link ammunition feed in place of the old canvas belt type which, if damp, tended to freeze at high altitudes, causing the gun to jam. The metal system had been invented by 'Naval 8's armament officer, Flt Lt Harry O'Hagan.

## SQUADRON MARKINGS

There were no specific squadron markings applied to 8 Naval Squadron's Triplanes, and official markings did not come into effect until August 1917, by which time the Triplanes had all been replaced with Camels. Names were painted in white either beneath the cockpit or – in somewhat larger characters – on the fuselage sides. Some Triplanes had white wheel covers and fins. Unlike 'Naval 1', the unit's Triplanes displayed British roundels on the fuselages.

Ed Crundell mentions the female names bestowed on the aircraft in his diary entry for 20 March 1917. He had christened his first 'Tripe' (N5439) *Whitfield* after his home village, but it was not popular;

'Soar told me nobody in "C" Flight liked the name *Whitfield*, and it was suggested I should change it. I was promised a brand new machine if I would select a name in accordance with the others in the flight. All the machines in "C" Flight had girls' names of their owner's fiancées. I told Soar I knew very few girls and did not know what name to choose. Soar had named his machine *Hilda*, and there was a *Gwen* and *Brenda*. It was suggested mine should be named *Doris*, so I exchanged Triplane N5439 *Whitfield* for Triplane N5464 *Doris*, and the name *Whitfield* was painted off N5439.

E D Crundell named his Triplane (N5439) after his home village of Whitfield, near Dover. However, he was asked to adopt a female name for his aircraft by his flight commander Reggie Soar, as this was the norm for Triplanes in 'C' Flight at that time (*Chaz Bowyer collection*)

53

# 'NAVAL 9'

Appropriately, 9 Naval Squadron was an off-shoot of 'Naval 8', being formed at St Pol on 1 February 1917. Initially flying a mix of Nieuport 17s and Pups that had been discarded by 8 Naval Squadron, 'Naval 9' had been established soon after 'Naval 8' had been relieved at the front by 3 Naval Squadron, the new unit – led by Sqn Cdr H Fawcett – being attached to 1 Naval Wing.

Unlike 1 and 8 Naval Squadrons, 'Naval 9' did not move to the British sector of the Western Front, the unit remaining on the North Sea coast. Based initially at St Pol, near Dunkirk, it moved a few miles up the coast to Furnes on 15 May. During this period the unit's pilots were charged with defending the Channel coast and allied shipping from German bombers. '9 Naval' also provided the fighter escort for reconnaissance flights being made by 2 Naval Squadron – this mission was usually undertaken by just three fighters.

While the new squadron was finding its feet, it was decided that as '9 Naval' grew in size it would supply pilots to the newly-formed 10 Naval Squadron. In essence, therefore, it became something of a reserve unit for 1, 8 and 10 Naval Squadrons, pending the formation of 12 Naval Squadron, which then became the service's dedicated training and reserve unit through which most naval fighter pilots passed on their way to frontline squadrons. The plan was for 'Naval 9' to eventually go to the British front in May to relieve 'Naval 3'. Although some records seem to indicate that Triplanes began arriving soon after its formation, a 9 Naval Squadron history noted the arrival of the first two Triplanes on 24 April.

As previously mentioned, on 15 May 10 Naval Squadron left on attachment to the RFC and 'Naval 9' took its place at Furnes aerodrome, where it came under the control of 4 Naval Wing. The unit still operated a mix of Pups and Triplanes, and it was the former which saw most of the early action. However, on 25 May three Triplanes and a Pup took off to intercept hostile aircraft which had raided Folkestone, in Kent. Fighters from both 4 and 9 Naval Squadrons made mostly inconclusive interceptions.

The next day Flt Sub-Lt O C LeBoutillier opened his score by claiming an LVG two-seater out of control off Ostend. This was followed by victory over an Albatros D III in the same area on 5 June – the day 22 Gotha bombers raided Sheerness, in Kent. They were intercepted by RFC and RNAS Home Defence units and, on their way back to the continent, by Dunkirk-based RNAS squadrons. Five Triplanes and two Pups were put up by 'Naval 9' at 1815 hrs, the fighters meeting about a dozen Albatros scouts off Ostend which had apparently been sortied to escort the bombers back over the coast. A scrap developed in which LeBoutillier, J W Pinder and Flt Lt J C Tanner each downed a D III 'out of control'.

John Pinder, from Deal, in Kent, thus gained his first kill (in N5462) – one of two Triplane victories he would achieve prior to flying Camels with 'Naval 9', 13 Naval/No 213 Sqn and, later still, No 45 Sqn. He finished the war with 17 kills and the DFC and Bar.

**American O C 'Boots' LeBoutillier of 9 Naval Squadron scored four victories while flying Triplanes and then went on to achieve six more with the Camel** *(Franks collection)*

J C Tanner was flying Triplane N5469 on 5 June, this aircraft having previously enjoyed success with 'Naval 8's' Robert Little at the controls – the Australian ace had scored his first four Triplane victories with it in April 1917. John Tanner, who had previously flown Pups with 'Naval 9', was injured in one of the last examples still flying with the squadron on 7 July during an encounter with a German two-seater. Having been shot up by his opponent, he spun in and crashed. Although he recovered from his injuries, Tanner was later killed in an Avro 504K on 1 August 1918 while serving as a captain with No 56 Training Depot Station.

H F Stackard claimed 15 victories with 9 Naval Squadron, although only one of these was scored flying a Triplane (N5451), on 8 June 1917. His remaining victories came on the Pup (two) and the Camel (12). Stackard is seen here sat in Camel B3883, which he claimed four victories with in September 1917 *(Franks collection)*

On 10 July 1917 another future Camel ace, Harold Francis Stackard, claimed an Albatros D III near Dixmude for his third kill – and his only one while flying the Triplane. The 9 Naval Squadron history records;

'Crossing the lines at Dixmude, he saw about six machines under AA fire over the coast at about 15,000 ft, but as the fire was very inaccurate he concluded that it was a "blind", and that the machines were hostile. This proved correct, and he attacked the nearest machine out of the sun head-on, firing a burst of about 20 rounds. He followed it down to 11,000 ft, firing all the time, whereupon the hostile machine side-slipped and went down in a spin entirely out of control.

'Another machine attacked the pilot from behind and Stackard had difficulty in getting away owing to the left-hand rudder wires being shot through. Finally, by means of a quick right-hand turn, he got behind the hostile machine and fired a burst, of which the tracers were seen to enter the fuselage and the EA went down apparently out of control. Flt Sub-Lt Stackard said that he was unable to continue the combat as his machine got

Oliver LeBoutillier made three victory claims while flying N5459 with 9 Naval Squadron *(Bruce/Leslie)*

into a spin, which he could not get out of until he had descended to 8000 ft. After great difficulty he headed the Triplane (N5451) homeward, partially losing control on two occasions, and when at 400 ft about half a mile to the east of the aerodrome, he lost control again and spun into the ground, escaping with minor injuries.'

Stackard would end the war with 15 kills, the final 12 of which were all scored while flying the Camel.

It was not until 15 June that 'Naval 9' was finally sent to the the British sector of the front, relieving 3 Naval Squadron at Flez, west of St

Quentin. There were few combats, though, for the unit initially suffered from a shortage of Triplanes – it had only nine on charge, of which five were unserviceable. The squadron's remaining aircraft were all Pups. Just one kill was scored whilst at Flez, J W Pinder claiming an Albatros scout on 7 July. 'Naval 9's' brief period with the RFC then came to an end.

On 10 July the squadron moved back north to Bray Dunes (Frontier Aerodrome), just up the coast from Dunkirk, where it re-equipped with Camels. Still flying Triplanes during the transition period, Flt Sub-Lt Edmund Pierce shot down an Albatros D V on 17 July, which he shared with four other pilots, including LeBoutillier. Pierce was already an ace on Pups with 3 Naval Squadron, and this represented his seventh claim.

Flt Cdr G G Simpson DSC, late of 'Naval 8' and now a flight leader with 'Naval 9', claimed a victory (in N5462) over a C type two-seater near Leffinge on the 24th. The first of the squadron's Camel victories came the following day, with Pinder also involved. On 28 July George Simpson and Flt Sub-Lt F J W Mellersh encountered a two-seater and sent it down 'out of control' over Middlekerke, the squadron having moved the previous day to Leffrinckhoucke, between Bray Dunes and Dunkirk.

Francis John Williamson Mellersh was born in September 1898, the son of a dentist who had his house and practice in Wimpole Street, London. Mellersh joined the RNAS in October 1916 and took his 'ticket' at Chingford in February 1917.

On 29 July Flt Lt A R Whealy and Flt Sub-Lt O C LeBoutillier each claimed an Albatros scout, Whealy's going down in flames and Oliver Boutillier's crashing at Leke at 0530 hrs. Fifty minutes later Whealy claimed a second Albatros near Ostend. LeBoutillier's Triplane score now stood at four, but his next victory did not come until 21 April 1918. That was the famous action between No 209 Sqn RAF (formerly 'Naval 9') and von Richthofen's 'Flying Circus' which ended with the death of the Red Baron.

This 9 Naval Squadron Triplane has the letter 'M' painted below the cockpit. If pilots personalised their machines, this scout might have been flown by future five-kill ace Francis Mellersh. The pilot standing in front of the aircraft has not been positively identified

F J W Mellersh claimed a single victory with Triplane N5377, and duly went on to become a Camel ace with No 209 Sqn *(Franks collection)*

'Boots' LeBoutillier stands in front of a 9 Naval Squadron Triplane, which appears to have a red and white diagonal fuselage stripe and broad white fuselage band. It is not known whether this is N5459 or N5484, both of which were flown by the American *(via L A Rogers)*

Hailing from New Jersey, in the USA, 'Boots' LeBoutillier had joined the RNAS in Canada in August 1916. He would end the war with ten victories to his credit, the last six of which were scored with Camels.

Fellow North American Arthur Whealy – 'Art' to his friends – had joined the RNAS in his native Toronto in 1915. He achieved five kills flying Pups with 3 and 9 Naval Squadrons, and then added two more with the Triplane before being given a Camel. Whealy would end the war with 27 victories to his credit, being awarded the DSC and Bar and the RAF's DFC in honour of his successes.

'Naval 9' took delivery of more Camels at the end of July, and by 4 August all the remaining Triplanes had been replaced. The unit had not achieved an awful lot with the Sopwith three-winger, but it had at least

A T Whealy, seen here flanked by fellow 3 Naval Squadron aces E T Hayne and H F Beamish, was another 'Naval 9' pilot to score modestly on Triplanes. Just two of his kills (claimed in N5490 in July 1917) were made while flying the type, although by war's end his tally stood at 27 victories, earning him a DSC and Bar and a DFC *(Franks collection)*

held its own. Only one pilot had been lost on operations, Flt Sub-Lt T R Shearer being killed when he failed to recover from a spin during an offensive patrol on 13 June 1917. While 'Naval 9' produced no actual Triplane aces, several pilots scored victories on their way to achieving 'acedom'. Whealy, already an ace, added one more scalp to his tally.

Future Canadian Camel ace A R Brown was a squadron pilot who later became very well known for his involvement in von Richthofen's last battle on 21 April 1918. Roy Brown had initially flown Pups with the unit, before switching to the Camel. According to his log-book, his only Triplane flights came on 8 June 1917, when he twice flew prototype N500 from the depot at Dunkirk. Three valves seized in the air and he landed after 15 minutes. Later, following repairs, Brown made a 15-minute flight to Handschoote.

## SQUADRON MARKINGS

Official markings were not applied to either Pups or Triplanes before late August 1917, by which time the Camels were at full strength. It is possible some carried individual letters or numbers to identify pilots in the air. There may have also been some personal designs. LeBoutillier, for instance, possibly used a Triplane with a red diagonal band, edged in white, painted from the cockpit to aft of the lower wing trailing edge. There was also a large white fuselage band behind the cockade. Certainly one Triplane carried the letter 'M' below the cockpit. 'Naval 9's' Camels displayed some interesting designs, and it seems inconceivable that this painting did not start during the Triplane period.

## IN THE MIDDLE EAST

While there were no aces created flying the sole Triplane sent to the Middle East, one pilot did open his score there, and another, who would achieve considerable fame after the war, also flew it. Aircraft N5431 was shipped out to the eastern Mediterranean in early 1917, being delivered to No 2 Wing RNAS in January. The wing's 'E' Flight used it (coded with the

**The sole Triplane sent out to the eastern Mediterranean, N5431 clashed with enemy aircraft on several occasions in 1917. It is seen here soon after its reassembly at Mikra Bay airfield, on the outskirts of the Greek city of Salonika, in January 1917 following its shipment from England. John Alcock, who flew the fighter extensively following its arrival in-theatre, poses in front of the machine** *(Bruce/Leslie)*

This photograph shows just how badly damaged N5431 was after Alcock ran it into a ditch at Mikra Bay on 26 March 1917. Miraculously, the pilot emerged unscathed *(Bruce/Leslie)*

Two years after seeing action in the the eastern Mediterranean in all manner of aircraft ranging in size from the Sopwith Triplane scout through to the Handley Page 0/100 bomber, John Alcock DSC undertook the transatlantic flight that was to make both him and A W Brown world famous

H T Mellings DSC and Bar DFC scored his four Triplane victories serving with 2 Naval Wing in the eastern Mediterranean in late 1917. Having increased his score to 15 victories flying Camels with 10 Naval Squadron on the Western Front, he was killed in action on 22 July 1918 *(via Mike O'Connor)*

letter 'L') until Flt Lt J W Alcock crashed the fighter at Mikra Bay airfield, in the Greek city of Salonika, on 26 March. The fighter was badly damaged when it over-turned after being run into a ditch.

John Alcock had learned to fly in 1912, and he subsequently joined the RNAS. After the war, he and Arthur Whitton Brown would be the first men to fly across the Atlantic in a Vickers Vimy. Both me were knighted in the wake of this outstanding feat.

Effectively written off, the Tri-plane was rebuilt at Mudros, on the Greek island of Lemnos in the Aegean Sea. By mid-May it was being flown by 'B' Squadron at Thermi, before moving on to 'C' Squadron at Imbros. On 25 May the fighter pursued an enemy aircraft over Suvla Bay, and shortly afterwards, in the hands of future ace Flt Sub-Lt H T Mellings, N5431 provided escort for a BE 2c reconnaissance aircraft flying in the same area. Mellings spotted a Halberstadt scout near Aivali and attacked it. During the ensuing scrap, the Halberstadt dived away in a tail-spin, smoke pouring from its engine. Mellings watched it fall down to a height of 3000 ft, where it was righted by its pilot. The naval pilot in turn spun the Triplane down after his foe, who flew low and fast back towards his airfield, pursued by Mellings. The fight eventually ended when the RNAS pilot was forced to break off his attack as the airfield defences opened fire. Later, the enemy erroneously reported that the BE 2c had been downed into the sea, and that the attacking Halberstadt had landed after a fight with a Triplane.

Although Alcock had primarily flown the Triplane when it first arrived in Greece, it was now Harold Thomas Mellings who was the fighter's principle pilot. A Shropshire lad, born in August 1897, Mellings joined the RNAS soon after the war started. Initially serving with 2 Naval Wing from October 1916, he had already seen some limited combat in a Bristol scout. On 30 September 1917, Mellings downed an Albatros W 4 fighter seaplane into the sea near Lemnos at 0800 hrs while flying the Triplane.

This was a famous action, with Mellings being sent off with John Alcock in a Camel and a Sopwith Pup flown by another pilot. The hostile force consisted of a two-seater observation machine escorted by two Albatros W 4s (effectively float-equipped D II scouts), which the Allied airmen nicknamed 'Bluebirds'. Mellings headed for the two-seater, but was engaged by one of the W 4s. Dodging this danger, he managed to fire at the second Albatros, but without result.

Alcock now attacked one of the fighters, but he stalled the Camel. As he fell away, he saw that his victim was streaming smoke. Mellings went for the other W 4, following the machine as it headed downwards. A further attack smashed part of the seaplane's port upper wing and wounded the pilot, who then hit the water and crashed. Mellings climbed back and had another go at the two-seater, leaving Alcock to finish off the remaining fighter before disengaging with an engine problem. Mellings and the Pup pilot continued to attack the two-seater, leaving it flying very low over the sea. The Germans reported the loss of FlugzeugObermaat Walter Krüger at Imbros on this date.

Despite Alcock's success in the Camel, ultimately, it would not prove to to be a good day for him. Having previously flown a Handley Page 0/100 bomber in combat, he took off later that same day in the machine

**Despite being all but written off in the 26 March 1917 crash, N5431 flew again after a major rebuild at Mudros, on the Greek island of Lemnos (strategically located between Greece and Turkey in the Aegean Sea). Note that in addition to the standard Vickers gun, Alcock also installed a Lewis gun above the cockpit during the fighter's reconstruction. Built with parts taken from other aircraft, Alcock called it his 'Sopwith Mouse' and also his 'Alcock A.1'** *(Bruce/Leslie)*

and raided Haida Pasha (Constantinople). However, the aircraft was hit by AA fire, forcing Alcock to ditch in the Gulf of Xeros, near Suvla Bay. The three crewmen survived, but had to swim ashore and were captured.

In November Mellings claimed three kills. On the 19th he downed an Albatros from 12,000 ft, which crashed into marshland near Zanoscw. This was followed by a Rumpler two-seater sent down in flames over Drama on the 25th. His last Triplane victory, over another Albatros scout, came four days later. For these efforts he received the DSC and the Greek War Cross. Returning to England, Mellings joined 10 Naval Squadron in 1918, flying Camels. By July he had been credited with 15 victories, and received a Bar to his DSC as well as the DFC. However, on 22 July Mellings was shot down and killed by Lutz Beckmann of *Jasta* 56.

There was only ever one 'Tripe' in the eastern Mediterranean, and contemporary reports indicate that parts of N5431 were used by John Alcock in the building of his unique single-seat fighter at Mudros. These were taken either from the damaged N5431 or were spares from the depot.

Devoid of its serial, the rebuilt N5431 is quite literally manhandled out onto the grass airfield at Mudros in anticipation of a combat patrol in the summer of 1917 *(Bruce/Leslie)*

## HOME DEFENCE

The few Sopwith Triplanes which saw service with RNAS Home Defence units were engaged in a number of actions, although none of the pilots involved were aces. However, one future ace was credited with a single victory while flying a Triplane in Britain – Rowan Heywood Daly.

Nineteen-year-old Daly spent much of the summer of 1917 flying obsolescent BE 2cs from Manston. On 7 July a large formation of Gotha bombers raided London in daylight, and on this occasion Daly was fortunate enough to be flying Triplane N5382. He used the fighter to good effect, downing a single Gotha. Daly also received praise for chasing another of the bombers across the

Triplane N5382 *THE OOSLUMBURD* sits on the grass at Manston, in Kent, in 1917. The aircraft was used by future ace Lt Bill Daly to intercept Gotha bombers on 7 July 1917

Sqn Cdr Charles Butler won the DSO and DSC for his tireless work on Home Defence duties with the Manston War Flight. He is believed to have flown more Home Defence sorties than any other pilot

Sopwith Triplanes were also used by the French Navy at St Pol for almost a year from late 1916. This example displays the number '9' on its top fuselage decking. Some French records note it as Clayton & Shuttleworth-built Triplane N5384 *(via Andy Thomas)*

Channel, his day's work earning him the DSC. Later that summer he went to France to join 10 Naval Squadron, by then flying Camels. Daly added two more victories to his score whilst flying with the unit, but it was not until 1919, when he engaged the Bolsheviks in Russia, that he became an ace. He scored a possible four victories during the campaign, taking his personal tally to seven. Awarded the DFC upon his return to Britain, Daly was killed in an aerial collision near Northampton in 1923.

Other Triplanes known to have been used by RNAS Home Defence units were N509 (flown by Flt Sub-Lts A C Burt and M A Harker), N5383 (flown by Burt and Flt Sub-Lt H C Lemon) and N535 (flown by Sqn Cdr G L Thompson). The description of these few actions would not be complete without referring to Sqn Cdr Charles H Butler, who was an RNAS flight commander at Westgate, in Kent, in early 1917. Predominantly flying Bristol Scouts and BE 2cs, Butler found himself at Manston in July, having become a squadron CO. During the spring and early summer he regularly flew Triplane N5424, which the RNAS had taken on strength in December 1916.

As far as is known, Butler flew more Home Defence sorties than any other RNAS or RFC pilot, and although he was never presented with the opportunity to become an ace, his actions won for him both the DSC and then the DSO. Flying N5424 on 5 June, he chased Gotha bombers back across the Channel to the Belgian coast. Butler fired at two but the results were uncertain due to cloud and mist. During the 7 July raid he, too, was credited with a Gotha bomber destroyed west of Ostende, and although it is now clear that the Germans only lost one aircraft in this attack despite several being claimed, Butler nevertheless had a successful engagement. On some of his sorties he went so far out over the water that he had to land at Dunkirk in order to refuel!

## FRENCH TRIPLANES

In late 1916 the French government ordered some Triplanes for its navy. They were allocated numbers F1 to F16 and sent to Dunkirk from late December 1916 – F11 to F16 did not arrive until June and July (see the

Henri Le Garrec, pictured with Triplane '14' at Dunkirk, gave the type its combat debut in French service on 16 February 1917. He later became the sole Triplane combat fatality when he was shot down in F15 by an unnamed pilot flying an Albatros scout from the crack *Jasta* 11 on 3 September 1917 (*Vacher via Lucien Morareau*)

Its cowling streaked with oil, French Triplane '3' sits at St Pol. The pilot in the cockpit does not look unlike Pierre Malvoisin (*L A Rogers*)

appendix for a full listing). The *Centre d'Aviation Maritime*, based at St Pol, operated a few SPAD VIIs and Nieuport 17s, as well as the Triplanes, during this period. Its unit COs were Lieutenant de Vaisseau (LV) Jean de Laborde (to 17 April 1917) and LV André Larfèvre.

The French enjoyed a few combat successes, the first on 16 February. Flying F1 (later N5384), Quartermaster Henri Le Garrec became involved in a dogfight with a German machine in company with another Triplane. He saw the enemy aircraft go down pouring smoke. Le Garrec, who came from Lorient, also flew F9 (marked 14, later N5388). One month and one day later, Sous-Lt Delesaue and another Triplane pilot engaged two German aircraft over Ypres. One was seen to go down in a spin and was duly claimed as a probable. This was followed on 12 April by a claim by Quartermaster Pierre Malvoisin over an Albatros two-seater.

Malvoisin, flying F5, claimed another enemy aircraft shot down between Nieuport and Dixmude on 3 June, and he followed this up by claiming three more 'victories'. The first came on 12 August when he damaged a German machine over Houthulst, followed by one of six Albatros scouts attacked over Dixmude on 4 September, and finally a Gotha over Dunkirk on the night of 30/31 October. Malvoisin reported that this latter aircraft had crashed into the sea, although on this occasion he was flying a SPAD VII. In all, Malvoisin was credited with four confirmed and three

probable victories – not all while flying Triplanes – which, in the RFC or RNAS, would have ranked him as a seven-victory ace.

Pierre Armand Malvoisin was born on 25 January 1897 in Paris, and he became a naval pilot on 11 August 1916 at Ambérieu as a *quatier-maître*. There were no marines in the French navy at the time, but some sailors were trained as infantrymen and called *fusiliers*. Awarded the *Croix de Guerre* and *Médaille Militaire* in November 1917, he was also made a *Chevalier de la Légion d'Honneur* the following month. Malvoisin was shot down while flying a Hanriot HD 2 seaplane on 26 May 1918, the Frenchman spending the rest of the war in captivity. The citation for his *Médaille Militaire* stated;

'*Quatier-maître, fusilier*, aviation pilot 385314 and admirable pilot, both spirited and driven. Always prepared for combat night or day. A model of courage and military discipline. Almost 200 operations over enemy lines. On 31 October 1917 he attacked and pursued an enemy aeroplane as far as its lines, where its destruction is more or less certain. This present nomination carries with it the award (palm) of the *Croix de Guerre.*'

Malvoisin's final rank was *second-maître* (petty officer second class), and he died on 2 October 1981 at Montrichard, Loir et Cher.

**Pierre Malvoisin in Triplane '10', which he used to engage an Albatros two-seater on 12 April 1917 *(Deturmény via Lucien Morareau)***

**These Triplanes were photographed at St Pol, near Dunkirk, soon after their delivery to the French Navy. The scout fourth from the left ('11') was the machine used by Pierre Malvoisin to claim his first official victory on 3 June 1917 *(L A Rogers)***

Fernand Vacher stands alongside Triplane '17'. He claimed three victories during World War 1, but none while flying the Triplane (*L Morareau*)

There is only one recorded loss of a French-flown Triplane in action – F15 (N5388) was shot down by a German fighter on 3 September 1917. The pilot, Quartermaster Garrec, being killed. This probably represented one of *Jasta* 11's two claims on this date, the other being a Triplane of 1 Naval Squadron. Curiously, German ace Friedrich Altemeier of *Jasta* 24 claimed a Triplane – his ninth victory – over Comines on 26 September. Records indicate that this was also the same N5388!

Fernand Charles René Vacher from Chabeuil, Drôme, learned to fly as a leading seaman air mechanic, and he often flew Triplane '17' (F8). He achieved three victories during the war, but none, it is believed, with a Triplane. Surviving the conflict as a petty officer second class, Vacher died in 1969.

## SQUADRON MARKINGS

Other than roundels and rudder stripes (applied in reverse to the RFC and RNAS colours), French Triplanes were marked only with individual white numbers painted on the fuselage ahead of the cockades. These were repeated on the top fuselage decking. Oddly, these numbers did not necessarily correspond with the French designation number, so that, for example, F8 was marked as '17', F9 was '14' and F15 was '12'.

## FLYING THE TRIPLANE

Cecil Lewis MC became well known after the war for his book *Sagittarius Rising*, which was first published in 1936 and has been rarely out of print since. Less well known is his *Farewell to Wings*, in which he describes many of the World War 1 aeroplanes he flew. Among them is the Sopwith Triplane, of which he wrote;

'What the fighter pilots wanted was something that could dive like a swallow and change direction like a bat. In a dogfight, manoeuvrability counted more than speed. It was up to the designers to meet service

requirements. The Triplane was a little beauty. The rotary engine, tank and pilot were all bunched close together so it could turn sideways or head over heals like a tumbler pigeon. Its three main planes carried all the area necessary for the load in such a small span that you could throw the Triplane from side to side like a leaf. Being from the Sopwith stable, the controls were nicely balanced and the machine handled like a polo pony.

'The "Tripe" vies with the Pup for pride of place in my heart for sheer flying pleasure. Both of them were underpowered, and never had the success the designs merited in service for this reason. The Triplane had one weakness – it couldn't really dive and, it was alleged, the wings came off if it was pointed at the ground with engine full on. But nobody, as far as I know, had tried this to the limit.

'The Triplane I flew had a 110-hp Clerget engine – a nice rotary job that could be throttled back like a stationary in-line engine. It was also so well balanced that it would fly hands off on the tail-trimmer, which other aircraft boasted they could do, but didn't. It could do more than this – set the engine at three-quarter throttle and wind the tail well back and the "Tripe" would loop indefinitely. I once did 21 loops in a row! But it was not in stunts like this that the charm of this aeroplane lay. It was perhaps the first really well-mannered and docile aircraft that responded immediately to the lightness of pressure on the controls. Equipped with a single Vickers gun firing through the prop, it proved a formidable adversary in a dogfight. Owing to the narrow chord of the three wings, the pilot's view was almost as good under one wing or the other. Altogether, the naval types did pretty well with the "Tripe" over France in 1917.'

Oliver Stewart MC, who had flown Pups with No 54 Sqn and later commanded the Aeroplane and Armament Experimental Establishment at Orfordness and Martlesham, wrote of the Triplane in *The Clouds Remember;*

A quarter of newly-delivered French Triplanes sit on the ground at St Pol in the summer of 1917. These aircraft were amongst the final batch of six Sopwith fighters that arrived in France in June and July 1917, some six months after the first 11 Triplanes had been transferred to French Navy control. Like the earlier machines, these late comers were also built by Clayton & Shuttleworth *(L A Rogers)*

**Right and below**
These detailed views of the Triplane's 'office' shows the spade grip control column and instruments, including a rev-counter, speedometer, altimeter, compass and clock. Note the Rotherham pump fixed to the starboard interplane strut in the photograph below. The padding above the spade grip in the shot to the right went some way to protecting the pilot's head from the machine gun's breech block in the event of a crash-landing *(Bruce/Leslie)*

'It would be difficult to analyse the feature in this machine that made it so attractive to fly. It seemed light and elegant, yet wiry. And there was the visual effect of the Triplane arrangement which made the pilot feel that he had unlimited quantities of lift available. The response to the controls was not of that lightning quickness exemplified by the Sopwith Camel, but it was by no means sluggish. At first it was thought that the Triplane could not be looped and flick-rolled with safety, but later it was made to do all the aerobatics of its time, and it did them well.'

Capt Vernon Brown was an exponent of aerobatics with the Triplane, and he showed it to be more than capable of performing a whole range of manoeuvres, and although it did not appear to perform the manoeuvres with the suddenness of the biplanes, it did so with infinite grace. He said;

'The Triplane spun rather slowly, and its flick roll was also rather slow compared with other machines of the time, but what it lacked in quickness it made up in the smoothness and grace of its movements. A Triplane looping looked like no other machine, and it gave the loops an individual quality. Irreverent pilots said it looked, when doing aerobatics, like an intoxicated flight of stairs.'

# 'NAVAL 10' AND 'BLACK FLIGHT'

The final RNAS fighting squadron to equip with Sopwith Triplanes was 10 Naval Squadron. Formed at St Pol on 12 February 1917 and commanded by Sqn Cdr C D Breese, it too remained in the north like 'Naval 9' (established just 11 days earlier at St Pol), flying patrols and escorts with Nieuport 12s and 17s and 1½ Strutters. The unit moved six miles inland to Furnes, in Belgium, on 27 March, and in early May it took delivery of its first Triplanes. Several weeks later, on the 15th, it moved south to Droglandt, where the unit came under the direct control of the RFC's 11th Wing. This was very much a frontline airfield, being due west of Ypres

Flt Cdr Raymond Collishaw had joined the squadron at Furnes on 26 April, by which time all its obsolete Nieuports had been totally replaced by Triplanes. 10 Naval Squadron also boasted a new CO in the form of Sqn Cdr B C Bell, a former 'Naval 3' flight leader.

Collishaw was already a seasoned veteran, having flown 1½ Strutters and Pups with 3 Wing and then 3 Naval Squadron since the previous autumn. He had also been shot down without serious injury just after Christmas.

Hailing from Nanaimo on Vancouver Island, in British Columbia, Collishaw was born on 22 November 1893 to British parents – his father had travelled from Wrexham, in Wales, to become one of the early gold prospectors. After leaving school, the young Collishaw had gone to sea in 1908 with the Canadian Fisheries Protection Service, first as a cabin boy and eventually rising to first officer. When war broke out he applied to join the RNAS and, while awaiting acceptance, went to the Curtiss flying school in Toronto to gain the necessary flying certificate.

There were many hurdles to surmount before Collishaw made it

Ray Collishaw commanded 10 Naval Squadron's 'B' Flight, which became famous as the 'Black Flight'. In all, Collishaw claimed 34 of his eventual 60 victories while flying the Triplane, thus becoming the type's top ace *(Franks collection)*

into combat. Because there were too many recruits at the Curtiss school, he did not learn to fly until he was sent to England in early 1916. Collishaw was eventually posted to 3 Naval Wing as a flight sub-lieutenant and sent to France to begin his war flying. By the time he moved to 'Naval 10' to take command of 'B' Flight, he had four combat victories to his name. Collishaw conducted his very first flight in a Sopwith Triplane just hours after arriving at Furnes, as he subsequently recorded in his book *Air Command*;

'The Triplane I found to be a delightful machine – in my estimation much preferable to the Pup. The machine was a private development of the Sopwith company, and the prototype made its appearance in mid-1916.

'The three-wing design was adopted to permit the pilot the widest possible field of vision, and also as a means of ensuring manoeuvrability. The middle wing was at the pilot's eye level, and interfered very little with his vision. All three wings had a narrow chord, and because of this the top and bottom wings blocked off less from the pilot's view than in the case of biplanes, which had wings of far greater chord, or measurement from leading to trailing edge. The Triplane was originally fitted with the 110 hp Clerget engine, but this was later replaced by the 130 hp Clerget. This more powerful engine gave it a speed of nearly 100 miles an hour at 15,000 ft, and it could climb to 10,000 ft in just under 12 minutes and had a ceiling approaching 20,000 ft.

'Apart from its manoeuvrability and its rate of climb, which was very good for its day, the Triplane's main virtue was the extreme altitude that it could attain, and its performance at these heights. Only about 150 Triplanes were built, but they made their presence felt on the Western Front to a remarkable degree. The Triplane's reign, if brilliant, was a relatively short one, and by the autumn of 1917 it was no longer considered a front-line machine.

'As in the case of all other aircraft, the Triplane had its weaknesses. It was not quite as fast as it might have been, and it could not match a machine such as the Albatros D III in a dive. Its main failing, though, by com-parison with the enemy fighters that it faced, was its armament. Like the Pup, it had but a single Vickers. The German fighters it was pitted against during 1917 had twin machine guns, and given anything like a comparable performance, it is hard to find a substitute for firepower. It may not have been feasible to have equipped the early Triplanes, which had the 110 hp Clerget, with twin Vickers, but I can think of no reason whythe 130 hp models, which "Naval 10" flew, could not have had two guns.

'Six experimental models were in fact fitted with twin Vickers, and I was fortunate enough to obtain one of these before leaving "Naval 10". When I brought it back to Droglandt it was greeted with mixed feelings. Some of the pilots considered that the extra firepower would be more than offset by a reduction in its performance at height as result of the added weight of the second machine gun, and its ammunition. Others, including myself, felt that a certain loss of performance would be acceptable in exchange for the extra gun. I found, in fact, that although there was a definite loss in performance above 10,000 ft, it was relatively slight, and having twice the firepower at my command that I had had before made a big difference.

'I continued to fly this machine – N533 – for the remainder of the time I was with "Naval 10", and wished very much that we had all been given twin-gun types long before. When I left the squadron, N533 was taken over by "Alex" (Capt W M Alexander).'

When Collishaw arrived at 10 Naval Squadron, he found it manned by in the main by fellow Canadians – as he noted in his book, there was something of a reunion of 3 Wing personnel. Other than the CO, 13 of the 15 pilots were Canadian! His own 'B' Flight was wholly Canadian, consisting of E V Reid, J E Sharman, G E Nash and W M Alexander – all these pilots would become Triplane aces. 'A' Flight comprised four Canadians and one Briton, as did 'C' Flight. Not long into the action, Collishaw's flight began to personalise its aircraft with the names *"BLACK*

Collishaw flew a number of Triplanes in 1917, including N533 seen here. Like all of his 'Tripes', he named the scout *'BLACK MARIA'*. Collishaw scored two victories with this aircraft on 27 July 1917 *(via Andy Thomas)*

Triplane N5492 was Collishaw's most successful *BLACK MARIA*, the Canadian claiming 18 victories with it. He then passed the scout onto G E Nash, who scored five more kills with it *(via Andy Thomas)*

*MARIA"* (N533 and N5490), *BLACK SHEEP* (N5492, which was originally flown by Nash but was later renamed *BLACK MARIA* when taken over by Collishaw), *BLACK DEATH* (N6307, flown by Sharman), *BLACK ROGER* (N5483, flown by Reid) and *BLACK PRINCE* (N5487, flown by Alexander). It became known as the 'Black Flight', but this was due to the fighters' names rather than the Triplanes' colour, although their noses were all black too. Collishaw told the author;

'When we began in 1917 we had three flights, and each aircraft was, respectively, coloured red, black and blue to denote "A", "B" or "C" Flight on the nose spinners and wheel covers. Initially, this was to aid the mechanics to identify their flight's aircraft when they landed because, being very light, the Triplanes needed to be held by the wingtips for support as we taxied in. With only the spinner and wheel covers painted black, it proved difficult to spot, so then we had the whole cowling and engine covering painted black, as well as the tail fin. "B" Flight soon began to be referred to as the "Black Flight" and, following this idea, I had the aircraft provided with names beginning with "Black". This was perpetuated by the press correspondents. The rest of the aircraft was in the normal RNAS dark khaki/green colour.'

As the squadron arrived at the front to support the hard-pressed RFC, it was having difficulty with guns jamming, which seemed to happen at the worst possible moment. This was partly due to improper tolerances, the parts having been machined with too close a fit. Once they became hot with firing they expanded and jammed. 'Naval 10's' engineers and armourers then began to use an abrasive which not only made the parts less tight and move more freely, but it also polished them. A new non-freezing oil helped, and so did the approach of warmer weather.

## 'BLACK FLIGHT'

Arriving at Droglandt, the squadron was thrown into the Battle of Messines, which began on 7 June 1917 and lasted until the 14th. In spite of a short period of uncertainty over the Triplane's structural reliability, imparted by the CO to the three flight commanders, operations got underway. As Bell informed his three leaders, they were stuck with the 'Tripe' and had to get on with it.

Ray Collishaw's 'Black Flight' had actually opened its scoring run within six days of arriving at Droglandt, Gerry Nash (in N5492) claiming an Albatros D III on 21 May. His victim crashed between Ypres and Staden. Then, on 1 June, came a victory by Flt Sub-Lt Reid in N5483, who shot down an Albatros two-seater west of Wervicq. A short time later the flight commander overcame gun problems to send an Albatros scout down in flames. The next day Collishaw, Alexander, Nash and Reid shared a two-seater sent down out of control over St Julien.

Ellis Vair Reid hailed from Belleville, Ontario. Born in October 1889, he was three years younger than Collishaw, although both men were older than Sharman, Nash and Alexander. After flight training, Reid had moved to 3 Wing, where he flew 1¹/₂ Strutters. Following his first successes with 'Naval 10', he went on to score a total of nine victories in June and a further ten in July. But on the day of his final victory, Reid's Triplane was brought down by AA fired from *K Flak* Unit 21. Shortly after his death came the announcement that he had been awarded the DSC.

**Ellis Vair Reid was second only to Ray Collishaw in terms of the number of Triplane victories he scored with 10 Naval Squadron, the Canadian claiming all 19 of his kills in just two months. Shot down by flak in late July 1917, Reid was posthumously awarded a DSC shortly after his death in action**

'Naval 10's' J E Sharman DSC and Bar also fell victim to flak, being shot down and killed on 22 July 1917. Seven of his eight victories were gained in Triplane N6307 *BLACK DEATH* (Franks collection)

John Edward Sharman was born in Oak Lake, Manitoba, in September 1892, and he joined the RNAS on 3 February 1916. He also flew $1^1/2$ Strutters in 3 Wing, completing at least 29 bombing missions before his posting to 'Naval 10'. Sharman had previously claimed one victory with 3 Wing prior to joining his new unit, and he added a further seven kills to his tally whilst serving under Collishaw. That earned him the DSC and command of 'C' Flight.

Like Reid, Sharman was also downed by anti-aircraft fire, his Triplane being struck on 22 July by a round fired from *Flak Batterie* 503. Some accounts maintain that he was brought down by Willi Reinhard of *Jasta* 11, who shot down a $1^1/2$ Strutter on this date. Others thought his Triplane had collapsed in the air. But in the event, the flak gunners took the credit. Sharman was engaged to an English lady at the time of his death, and a few years ago the author met her daughter from a subsequent marriage, whose mother had kept a number of photos of her former fiancée, one of which appears on the page opposite.

Triplane N5364 of 10 Naval Squadron was shot down by Helmut Dilthey of *Jasta* 27 on 24 July 1917. In its final dive to earth all three of its wings folded back (T Mellor-Ellis collection)

**Factory-finish view of N5364 at Farnborough in May 1917. This aircraft was one of 47 built by sub-contractor Clayton & Shuttleworth (RAE Farnborough)**

**W M Alexander DSC, pictured just before he joined the RNAS in 1916, was 'Naval 10's' third-ranking Triplane ace with ten kills. He survived the deadly summer of 1917 and finished the war with a tally of 22 victories, the remaining 12 being scored on Camels (Franks collection)**

Gerald Ewart Nash, from Stoney Creek, was born in May 1896 and joined the RNAS in April 1916. He was posted to 'Naval 10' after service with 3 Wing, and his victory tally had reached six by 7 June. However, on the 26th he was shot down by Karl Allmenröder of *Jasta* 11, becoming the German ace's 29th victim, and a PoW. During World War 2, Gerry Nash served in the RCAF, retiring as a group captain in 1945. He died on 10 April 1976, a month short of his 80th birthday.

William Melville Alexander was born November 1897 and came from Toronto, joining the RNAS in 1916 to 'complete the set' within 'B' Flight, as he too had been with 3 Wing. He had actually learned to fly at the Stinson School in San Antonio, Texas, where he was instructed by Eddie Stinson himself. The latter individual established the Stinson company in the 1920s, and his biplane trainers became well known to a later generation of fighter and bomber pilots during World War 2. As a matter of interest, Stinson's sister Katie was one of the first two women pilots in North America, the other being Ruth Law. Katie actually started the Stinson School and, having arrived in Toronto during the early war years, advertised its services in the newspapers. Alexander was one of many would-be aviators who applied in November 1915.

When he tried to join the RNAS he was interviewed by Adm Charles Kingsmill, head of the Canadian naval service. An officer remembered for his naval beard and Victorian manner, Kingsmill also interviewed Ray Collishaw. A short while later Alexander received a letter to say he was too young – he was still not quite 18 – but within a few days, having passed his 18th birthday, he encountered the admiral again. Learning that Alexander had applied to learn to fly in Texas, Kingsmill relented and said that he would take him – provided, presumably, that he got his license.

73

H J T Saint joined 10 Naval Squadron in July 1917 and eventually became a flight commander

Saint used Triplane N6295 'B' to claim two of his four Triplane victories in August 1917. His final wartime tally reached seven kills (*via Andy Thomas*)

N6295's white 'B' code letter and serial are both clearly visible in this photograph

Flying Triplanes with 'Naval 10', he scored ten victories between June and August, and continued this success after the Camel's arrival. Not that he got off to a good start with the Triplane, however, for his log-book describes his first, somewhat undistinguished, encounter with the Sopwith scout;

'28 April 1917, 17-minute practice flight. First flight in Triplane. Turned up on nose on landing, breaking prop and denting cowling.'

Two days later, though, Alexander experienced his first combat, flying N5483;

'30 April 1917. Attacked by large hostile machines, my own machine being hit in several places. Made steep climbing turn and opened fire with about 50 rounds. The hostile machine then dived away to the left.'

Flying N5487 on 6 July on an Offensive Patrol, he recorded;

'Encountered about 25 EA scouts near Deulemont – killed pilot of one and drove another down into sideslip and nosedive. Was then forced to dive to get away from two others.'

Despite being firm in his belief that he had hit, and killed, the pilot of the first Albatros, Alexander was credited with only two scouts 'out of control'. In later life he recalled this first victory, and how he had opened fire on his target from a distance of just 40 ft;

'I saw the bullets streaming right into the cockpit. I was very excited. Over the trenches our nerves were so taut that when we got back, landed and lifted our goggles, it was like having a 100-lb weight eased off your back.'

Both eight-victory aces (and each with seven kills on the Triplane), Canadians John Sharman (left) and John Page of 10 Naval Squadron were both killed on 22 July 1917. Sharman fell to flak and Page was almost certainly shot down by *Jasta* 11 ace Ltn Otto Brauneck

The graves of Flt Cdr J E Sharman and Flt Lt J A Page of 10 Naval Squadron, who both died on 22 July 1917 aged 24. They are buried side-by-side at Pont-du-Hem Cemetery in France *(N Franks)*

Of the dogfights, he recalled 'the clatter of his engine, the high pop-pop-popping of the machine gun and the flic-flic-flic as slugs tore through his aircraft's fabric.'

Alexander's last Triplane combat took place on the evening of 21 August, in N6302, as he recalled;

'OP, escorting DH 4s. Great EA activity. Bagged one and was forced to fight my way out from Menin with five EA scouts.'

By late May 1918, when the unit had become No 210 Sqn, his score had risen to 22, and he had received the DSC. Alexander died in Canada on 4 October 1988 at the age of 90. In 1973 he told a newspaper that he credited his longevity (he was then a mere 76) to good Scotch, good cigars and porridge! He was often referred to as 'Mel', 'Alex' or 'Alec'.

During a taped conversation with fellow RNAS fighter pilot A W 'Nick' Carter in 1970, Alexander mentioned the Triplane's initial structural trouble;

'You really came down in the Triplane. God, Nick, when I look back and I think about those Triplanes, holy jumping! We had a lot of them fold up, but God knows why we didn't have a lot more of them do so. The ones we know folded up

**Flt Cdr A W Carter DSC served as 'A' Flight commander with 10 Naval Squadron after seeing considerable action flying Pups with 'Naval 3'. Four of his eventual 17 victories were claimed on Triplane N6302** *(Bruce/Leslie)*

over the lines were Les Parker and Sharman (Carter then interrupted, saying he thought Sharman was hit by AA fire). We know he was in a dogfight. He was going down in a dive, and the fellows that were with him gave the report that all of a sudden his wings came off. Look at the number of fellows that just folded up on our side of the line – Art Dissette, Bill Oliver, Ted Glasgow. Those were the ones we knew about. The Triplane only had one set of flying wires.'

As the conversation continued, Carter recalled that when he was with the squadron he added an extra set of wires to the wings on his Triplanes, as did Collishaw. Alexander said he put on a cable wire. Carter commented that it slowed the aircraft down a bit, but it certainly strengthened them. Alexander continued;

'There were two kinds of Sopwiths. The one built by Sopwith had the flying wires streamlined. They were both five-eighths of an inch in width. Then there was another outfit called the Clayton company (Clayton & Shuttleworth, who built 47 Triplanes). They had a sub-contract to build the aircraft, but their wires were only three-eighths of an inch wide. They were the ones that were always folding up.

'I was on leave at the end of August 1917, having left the Triplanes at the front, and when I got back we had Camels. They had broken up 6 Naval Squadron, and we got about six pilots from the unit – our casualties were so bad at the time that we couldn't make do with replacements, so they broke up "Naval 6". All our surviving Triplanes had in turn been passed on to 1 Naval Squadron.'

Alfred William Carter – usually known as 'Nick' – was born in Calgary, Alberta, in April 1894. He joined the RNAS in May 1916 after service with the Canadian Army's Queen's University Battery. Knowing it was preferable to be able to fly before attempting to join the air service, he and some friends had gone to Florida in the hope of finding someone to teach them. They were unlucky and had to return north. However, Carter did eventually learn to fly, and when finally posted to France he, too, went to 3 Wing. In March 1917 he moved to 3 Naval Squadron, which was then flying Pups. Carter had already claimed five victories by the time he was posted to 'Naval 10'. As he remarked during the 1970 conversation;

'I went to No 3 on Pups, and we had quite a session on those machines. It was an excellent squadron. Finally, 3 naval Squadron was sent up the coast for a rest and, my God, I'd no sooner got to the coast than the flight commander came and said, "Nick, you're posted to No 10 as flight commander and I'm sending you on ten days' leave". I took over "A" Flight. Ted Sharman was the other flight commander. Everyone laughed like hell at me. "A" Flight had had two flight commanders killed, and they said, "Go on, Nick, you're the third!"

'"Colly" and Ted Sharman used to fight like nobody's business in our flight commander's hut about who was going to have these French-built Clerget engines. Well, of course, the flight commander had a French engine. I went down to Nelson, the engineering officer, and I said, "Look, these fellows are fighting to beat the band about these engines. Let's put it over on them and you slip all the French Clergets into my flight". By golly, Collishaw and Sharman woke up one time and found that I had all the French engines. They were hopping mad! They were really upset about that.'

Nick Carter added four victories to his score while flying Triplanes, and by June 1918 had boosted his tally to 17 with the Camel – he had also won a DSC by then. In the final weeks of the war he commanded No 210 Sqn RAF. Air Marshal Carter died in Canada on 17 December 1986.

## THE OTHER FLIGHTS

When first formed, 'Naval 10's' 'A' Flight was comprised of Flt Sub-Lts P C Neil, C E Pattison, L H Parker, K G Boyd and A B Holcroft, all of whom were Canadians bar Holcroft. When Boyd left the unit in July 1917, he was the last survivor of the original five, the rest having become casualties. 'C' Flight – Flt Sub-Lts A C Dissette, J A Page, J H Keene, D F FitzGibbon and Q S Sherriff – who again reflected the four-to-one ratio in favour of Canadian pilots, with FitzGibbon being the only Briton. And it was he who survived the early summer, with two of the others being killed, a third pilot being wounded and the fourth leaving in July. A few victories were scored by these flights, with Page and Dissette opening their accounts by sending an Aviatik two-seater down out of control on 1 June 1917. Only Page and FitzGibbon eventually became aces, however.

John Albert Page was born in Brockville, Ontario, in July 1893. His first operational role was with Home Defence, flying from Yarmouth Royal Naval Air Station in early 1916. Moving to France, Page served with 3 Naval Squadron before being posted to 'Naval 10' in April 1917. During June he achieved four victories, followed by a fifth on 7 July. Then, on the 22nd, Page was involved in a battle in which two German fighters were seen to go down – one was out of control, while the other was seen to crash. J A Page failed to return.

He was claimed by Ltn Otto Brauneck of *Jasta* 11, becoming the German's tenth, and final, victory. It was to be a short-lived triumph, as four days later Brauneck fell to the guns of Capt N W W Webb MC of No

Desmond FitzGibbon DSC of 'Naval 10' claimed eight victories, five of which were scored with the Triplane in the summer of 1917 (*E F Cheesman via M Westrop*)

*Jasta* 4's Kurt Wüsthoff (standing below the Vickers gun) poses in front of N5429, which represented his 15th victory when he forced Flt Sub-Lt J R Wilford down on 13 September 1917. The aircraft displays the number '2' on its fuselage, and would also have shown 'Naval 1's' two small vertical white bars between the number and the serial (*L A Rogers*)

70 Sqn. He was Noel Webb's ninth victim. As previously mentioned in this chapter, 10 Naval Squadron also lost 'B' Flight's eight-kill ace John Sharman on 22 July, thus inflicting a double blow on the unit.

Desmond Fitzgerald FitzGibbon was born in Hampstead, north London, on 1 November 1890, and he had joined the RNAS on 28 May 1916 and qualified as a pilot at Cranwell on 14 August. He claimed five victories between 5 June and 25 August and then added three more in September following the arrival of the Camel. FitzGibbon was sent home to rest that autumn, where he was awarded the DSC.

George Leonard Trapp was yet another of 'Naval 10's' Canucks. Born in New Westminster, near Vancouver, British Columbia, in July 1894, he joined the RNAS in 1916 and was posted to 10 Naval Squadron. Trapp first three victories were claimed while flying Triplanes in August, and he added two more with the Camel in September. He was, however, killed in action on 12 November when shot down by Oblt Bruno Justinius of Bavarian *Jasta* 35.

Trapp was one of three brothers to die serving with the RNAS, Stanley Valentine Trapp having been lost with 8 Naval Squadron in December 1916 when his Pup shed its wings during a test flight over his own aerodrome. He was 26. Brother Donovan, aged 23, was killed flying an SE 5a with No 85 Sqn RAF on 19 September 1918, his demise probably representing an unconfirmed claim made by Uffz Murat Schumm. Had this victory been confirmed, Schumm would have ended the war as a five-victory ace.

On leave in Canada, Ray Collishaw visited the Trapp family, and as a result of this meeting he subsequently married Neita, one of two daughters. Although they became engaged, it was six years before they could find time to marry. Trapp's name was put forward for a posthumous award, but it was declined, as the following exchange of correspondence makes clear;

This photograph of N5429 was taken soon after it had been marked with German national insignia. The 'Naval 1' scout had previously served with both 10 and 8 Naval Squadrons, and 'Naval 10's' H W Taylor claimed at least two victories while flying it *(Greg VanWyngarden)*

George Trapp of 10 Naval Squadron claimed three of his six victories on Triplanes. He was killed in action flying a Camel on 12 November 1917 *(E F Cheesman via M Westrop)*

N5366 shows a variation in the way serial numbers were applied to Triplanes. John Sharman flew this aircraft on occasion, and George Trapp scored his third, and last, Triplane victory with it on 21 August 1917 *(Bruce/Leslie)*

To: Commanding Officer 14th Wing RFC

I wish to bring to your notice the name of Acting Flt Cdr G L Trapp, who was killed in an air combat on the 12th instant, as especially deserving of the DSC.

This pilot has rendered very valuable service since joining the Squadron on 14 July 1917. His work has always been most steady and consistent, and he achieved a considerable number of material successes of which a note is appended.

12 August: Over Roulers, pilot attacked several EA scouts out of a formation of five and eventually drove one down completely out of control.

Triplane N5357 'K', flown by Flt Sub-Lt R L Kent (who became a PoW) of 10 Naval Squadron, was shot down over Comines by Walter Blume of *Jasta* 26 on 11 July 1917. Note that the roundel and serial number have been cut out as souvenirs by German troops. It is believed that the original crash landed with the Triplane on its back *(T Mellor-Ellis collection)*

17 August: In a general engagement near Ledeghem with six Albatros scouts, he fired 40 rounds into one from close range and drove it down out of control.

21 August: Near Menin, in another general engagement, pilot drove one Albatros scout down out of control.

9 September: East of Zonnebeke, pilot attacked an EA scout, which dived from a formation above, and fired 120 rounds from about 75 yards behind its tail. EA went down out of control. The fall of this machine was confirmed by artillery observation.

28 September: East of Moorslede, pilot attacked one of four Albatros scouts and fired 150 rounds from close range. EA went down entirely out of control and was observed to crash by Flt Cdr Alexander, who had gone down low in pursuit of another machine.

12 November: In the morning of this day, pilot and Flt Sub-Lt Beattie attacked an EA two-seater near Couckelaere. Pilot fired 400 rounds and followed EA down to 2000 ft, when it fell out of control and turned over on its back. In the afternoon of this day, pilot was killed while engaging an enemy two-seater machine.

In the field

R F Redpath

November 14, 1917
Commanding Officer
Naval Squadron No 10'
To: Headquarters
RFC

Forwarded and strongly recommended.

Acting Flt Lt G L Trapp's example as a patrol leader was invaluable. He is a great loss.

Another view of N5357, which has been righted and is now being wheeled away by German mechanics. This picture was turned into a postcard in Germany *(T Mellor-Ellis)*

In the field
P R Joubert

November 15, 1917
Lt-Col
Commanding XIVth Wing, RFC
To: Headquarters
14th Wing RFC
Your AC 269 of the 15th instant.
It is regretted that with the exception of the Victoria Cross, posthumous honours are not awarded.
Headquarters RFC
F Festing
Brig-Gen
DAG
17 November 1917

## MARKINGS

All uppersurfaces of 10 Naval Squadron's Triplanes were painted in standard PC10 khaki/green camouflage, while wings and fuselage undersurfaces were clear doped. To identify aircraft on the ground and in the air, 'A' Flight machines had red cowlings and metal panels, 'B' Flight had black and 'C' Flight blue. Wheel covers and tail fins were similarly coloured as appropriate. 'B' Flight aircraft also displayed names in white paint beneath and just forward of the cockpit sides, the mechanics having designed and produced stencils for this purpose. Later, individual letters were painted on some fuselages in white with the pilot's surname initial, such as 'C' for Collishaw and 'S' for Sharman.

## COMBATS WITH THE 'CIRCUS'

June 1917 saw 10 Naval Squadron involved in an increasing number of combats with Manfred von Richthofen's new *Jagdesgeschwader* Nr I. The RFC called it the 'Circus' because it moved from place to place along the front. Von Richthofen, until recently leader of *Jasta* 11, now had four *Jagdstaffeln* under his command – *Jastas* 4, 6, 10 and 11. But this did not mean that he flew at the head of all four units all the time. The grouping was due more to administrative expediency than to the need to operate as a large force. His four *Jasta* commanders at this time were aces Kurt von Doring, Eduard Dostler, Albert Dossenbach and Karl Allmenröder. The group was based at airfields near Courtrai, on the 4th German Army sector, while 'Naval 10' flew from Droglandt, west of Ypres. In his book, Ray Collishaw vividly described one of his flight's first combats on 1 June;

'So far as I was concerned, my first action out of Droglandt was on 31 May, when the flight I was leading came across two enemy aircraft engaged in directing German artillery fire. They both got away, but we had the satisfaction of knowing that we had spoilt their game.

'My first real scrap came the following day, 1 June, when I led "B" Flight in full strength – Reid, Sharman, Nash and Alexander were the others – on a distant offensive patrol that took us over the Menin area. The *Jastas* seemed to be out in force, and we encountered enemy machines on three separate occasions during the patrol, which lasted for nearly two-and-a-half hours. One of the formations that we ran into was over Menin – three Albatros D IIIs – and they were at about 14,000 ft, a couple of thousand feet below us. I pushed my stick forward and the rest of "B" Flight followed as we dived on them in formation. I singled one of them out, but was thwarted when my gun jammed. We broke formation and the usual dogfight ensued, and I was able to find a moment or two of breathing space to clear my gun.

'The fight drifted down, and we were at about 8000 ft when I managed to get into position again for a shot on another of the enemy, and closed to 30 yards or so before firing. My antagonist was flying a machine that was painted in a mottled effect and which bore a large "L" on the side of its fuselage. As I fired, I saw my tracers go right into him and he went down out of control, bursting into flames as he did so. He crashed just south of Wervicq, not far from Menin. Gerry Nash sent one down in the same scrap. He saw his tracers hit and the Albatros went down in a spin. Neither he nor any of the rest of us, though, were able to determine whether it pulled out before crashing.

'On the return we encountered three more of the enemy – one of them an Albatros two-seater – to the east of Armentières. I dived on the two-seater, but was again baulked by gun trouble. Ellis Reid, however, got away a short burst at long range and one of his tracers went right into the head of the gunner in the rear cockpit. Ellis pulled up and then dived again, and this time his fire went straight into the neck of the pilot. The last we saw of the two-seater, it was going down in a near vertical dive, and I think there was very little chance that it ever pulled out.'

Despite this account, combat for the RNAS pilots in the summer of 1917 was certainly not all one-sided in favour of 'Naval 10'. The first two weeks of June saw the loss of three of pilots (Flt Sub-Lts I S Dissette, P G McNeil and L H Parker) on the 2nd, 3rd and 14th to the 'Circus'. Karl Allmenröder and Gisbert-Wilhelm Groos of *Jasta* 11 brought down two more – Flt Sub-Lts A B Holcroft and R G Saunders – on the 24th. Allmenröder then downed Gerry Nash on the 25th for his 29th victory. On 9 June Collishaw himself nearly became another combat statistic, as he recorded;

'This day saw the end of N5490, the Triplane that I had flown on most of my patrols since joining "Naval 10", and it was very nearly the end of

Triplane N5358, flown by Flt Sub-Lt A B Holcroft of 'Naval 10', was downed on 24 June 1917 by Karl Allmenröder of *Jasta* 11. This represented his 28th victory *(Bruce/Leslie)*

The war's leading Triplane ace with 34 kills, Ray Collishaw went on to fly Camels with No 210 Sqn and take his final score to 60 victories by the time of the Armistice

Collishaw. I took off from Droglandt at 0500 hrs with a two-flight patrol detailed to cover the area east of Ypres, and we had hardly crossed the lines when we ran into a formation of Albatros D IIIs. As usual, they were below our altitude, and we dived on them, going down from 17,000 ft. I got on the tail of one of them and, although the German pilot went into a series of tight turns, my Triplane was able to turn even more tightly. It looked like another sure victory, and I had just got his tail into my sights, and was about to open fire, when a devastating stream of bullets smashed into my cockpit. They came at me from out of the sun. His attack left me unscathed but shattered my controls. I was quite helpless.

'I could do nothing at all to control my machine, which fell off on one wing and then went into a hair-raising series of cartwheels and wild swoops and dives. I was absolutely terrified at first, but this gave way to a dulled sort of resignation, and I can recall thinking rather wistfully how nice it would be to have a parachute.

'We had been at around 16,000 ft when my machine was damaged, and the descent took some 15 minutes, although it seemed much longer than that. We fell closer and closer to the ground and, just before smashing into a hillside, the Triplane took it in its mind to try one final swoop, and that saved me. We hit with a tremendous crash and the Triplane folded into a mass of wreckage, but I was left intact with no more than bruises and a determination that never, never again would I let anyone come at me out of the sun.'

On 24 June Ray Collishaw claimed one Albatros scout destroyed, saying it was bright red in colour. His combat report describes the action, timed at 0805 hrs (German time being one hour ahead at this stage);

'Escorting two DH 4s of No 57 Sqn – at 11,000 ft – in the vicinity of Moorslede, four EA scouts attacked the DHs and I closed immediately on one, which got into a spin. I then fired at an EA on one DH's tail. While engaged with it, I observed Flt Sub-Lt Alexander attack one on the other DH's tail. Flt Sub-Lt Alexander got away towards the lines with a gun jam. I closed to about 25 yards on EA's tail before I got in position to fire. After about 40 rounds, the enemy machine went out of control and I saw the wings come off one side. The machine crashed near the road from

Heinrich Kroll of *Jasta* 24 claimed three Triplanes during his career as a fighter pilot, although two of these seem dubious. He survived the war with a score of 33 victories

Gisbert-Wilhelm Groos of *Jasta* 11 also claimed three British machines, although all of his were positive kills

Moorslede to Passchendaele. About this time we were attacked by 15 additional scouts, and I was chased by four of them down to the ground and was only able to get across the lines at about 50 ft.'

On the 26th, Karl Allmenröder brought down a Nieuport 17 of No 1 Sqn RFC to score his 30th victory. It was also to be his last. Early the next day he fell near Zillebeke, crashing into 'no man's land'. German soldiers retrieved Allmenröder's smashed body that evening.

In later life, Ray Collishaw became quite an enthusiastic aviation historian, and the author corresponded with him for some time. He was very knowledgeable, having known personally so many of the war's RFC, RNAS and RAF pilots. He had been leading a 'Naval 10' patrol on 27 June, and had fired at long range at a group of Albatros scouts, so after the war, when it became known that the leader of *Jasta* 11 had fallen that day, he wondered if it had been his long-distance shot which had scored the fatal hit. In 1968 Collishaw wrote;

'Indecisive combats were common on the Ypres Front in the summer of 1917 – a period of the hottest air superiority dispute in the war. What happened on the 27th was that I led my flight of No 10 Naval Squadron scouts over the lines at about 15,000 ft, and I found that we were stationed between two hostile formations, one below and one above – a kind of meat sandwich. We flew in these conditions for some time. I now know that *Jasta* 11 was flying in two *ketten* (sub flights), one above us and the other below us. All three formations were climbing hard, so the formations sustained their relative positions. I know that we were in a dangerous position because if the upper *Jasta* 11 formation attacked us, we should almost certainly get involved with the lower formation. I decided, therefore, to get out of the picture by diving to escape to the westward, but as we did so, I proposed to try to shoot up the lower formation on the way out. So I made the signal to my companions to attack.

'When I got to about 10,000 ft above the lower formation, I opened fire at long range on the leading Albatros. I had hardly begun to fire before I felt the impact of bullets on my aircraft – the upper *kette* had dived – so I took violent evasive action and got out of the way fast. As I had fired at my target, I had noticed that it immediately moved in a peculiar manner, but I thought nothing of it at the time, as it seemed to be performing simple avoiding action that was in common use at the time.

'Flt Sub-Lt Nash, on becoming a PoW, was imprisoned, temporarily, in a village near to where Allmenröder fell, and when he heard its local church bells ringing, his German guard told him that the tolling was for Allmenröder, who had been shot down by a Sopwith Triplane squadron. Of course, I did not know anything about this until Nash returned to England in 1919.'

Many years afterwards, Collishaw related that he was in touch with Gisbert-Wilhelm Groos of *Jasta* 11, who seemed to confirm the story about the Triplanes and his leader falling. However, it is now accepted that the German's Albatros had been the victim of anti-aircraft fire, and in any event Collishaw's action was timed at 1720 hrs. By that time Allmenröder had been lying dead between the trenches for more than seven hours.

One result of these actions between JG I and 'Naval 10' was that Manfred von Richthofen became intrigued with the triplane design and

Freidrich Altemeier, also of *Jasta* 24, was yet another German pilot to claim three Triplanes in 1917 – the validity of at least one of these kills remains uncertain. He finished the war with 21 victories to his credit

concept. Indeed, the German aircraft industry had already noted the three-winged fighter's presence at the front since early in the year, and several companies had put forward designs. However, it was the Fokker company which produced the one that was to become legendary as the Dr I Triplane. Once he had started flying it, von Richthofen favoured the Fokker Driedecker, and he used it for a short period in September 1917 and then from March 1918 until his death the following month. As a result, the Dr I has come to symbolise aerial warfare in World War 1.

The Red Baron flew his new Fokker Triplane (F I 102/17) for the first time in action on the morning of 1 September 1917. It was a day of low clouds and rain, but with bright intervals later. At 0750 hrs, near Zonnebecke, he attacked an RE 8 observation machine of No 6 Sqn RFC. The British crew were somewhat perplexed as the Triplane came towards them, for the only machines of this type familiar to them were the naval Sopwiths. But the Triplane opened fire and they were shot down, the observer being killed, while the badly wounded pilot was taken prisoner.

As von Richthofen stated in his combat report;

'Apparently, the opponent had mistaken me for an English Triplane because the observer in the machine stood upright without making a move for his machine gun.'

It was clear that as the Allied Triplane was ending its time at the front, that of the German one was just beginning.

# APPENDICES

## Triplane Aces

| Name | Squadron/s | Claims on Type | War Total |
|------|-----------|----------------|-----------|
| Maj R Collishaw | 10 | 34 | 60 |
| Capt R A Little | 8 | 24 | 47 |
| Maj C D Booker | 8 | 21 | 29 |
| Flt Sub-Lt E V Reid | 10 | 19 | 19 |
| Flt Lt R P Minifie | 1 | 17 | 21 |
| Maj R S Dallas | 1 | 16 | 32 |
| Capt W M Alexander | 10 | 10 | 22 |
| Maj R J O Compston | 8 | 9 | 25 |
| Maj T F N Gerrard | 1 | 8 | 10 |
| Capt S W Rosevear | 1 | 8 | 25 |
| Capt R R Soar | 8 | 8 | 12 |
| Flt Lt J A Page | 10 | 7 | 8 |
| Flt Cdr J E Sharman | 10 | 7 | 8 |
| Capt G G Simpson | 8/9 | 7 | 8 |
| Flt Sub-Lt T G Culling | 1 | 6 | 6 |
| Flt Cdr C A Eyre | 1 | 6 | 6 |
| Capt S M Kinkead | 1 | 6 | 35 |
| Capt F H M Maynard | 1 | 6 | 6 |
| Flt Lt G E Nash | 10 | 6 | 6 |
| Lt A G A Spence | 1 | 6 | 9 |
| Maj A R Arnold | 8 | 5 | 5 |
| Flt Lt D F FitzGibbon | 10 | 5 | 8 |
| Capt H V Rowley | 1 | 5 | 9 |

## Aces who scored victories flying the Triplane

| Name | Squadron | Claims on Type | War Total |
|------|----------|----------------|-----------|
| Maj A W Carter | 10 | 4 | 17 |
| Capt O C LeBoutillier | 9 | 4 | 10 |
| Capt H T Mellings | 2 Wg | 4 | 15 |
| Capt C B Ridley | 1 | 4 | 11 |
| Capt H J T Saint | 10 | 4 | 7 |
| Capt E D Crundell | 8 | 3 | 7 |
| Capt R McDonald | 8 | 3 | 8 |
| Flt Cdr P A Johnston | 8 | 3 | 6 |
| Flt Lt G L Trapp | 10 | 3 | 6 |
| Capt R R Thornely | 8 | 3 (and possibly 2 more) | 9 |
| Capt A T Whealy | 9 | 2 | 27 |
| Capt J W Pinder | 9 | 2 | 17 |
| Lt R H Daly | Home Defence | 1 | 7 |
| Capt J H Forman | 1 | 1 | 9 |
| Capt F J W Mellersh | 9 | 1 | 5 |
| Maj R B Munday | 8 | 1 | 9 |
| Flt Sub-Lt H F Stackard | 9 | 1 | 15 |

# Ace Triplanes

| Serial Number/Nickname | Sqn/s | Score | Pilot/s |
|---|---|---|---|
| N5492 *BLACK MARIA* | 10 | 23 | R Collishaw (18) and G E Nash (5) |
| N5493 *BLYMP* | 8 | 20 | R A Little |
| N5482 *MAUD* | 8 | 17 | C D Booker |
| N5483 *BLACK ROGER* | 10 | 17 | E V Reid |
| N5490 *BLACK MARIA* | 10 | 14 | R Collishaw |
| N5436 (coded 'C') | 1 | 13 | R S Dallas (11) and C B Ridley (2) |
| N5465 | 1/8 | 12 | R R Thornely (5), E D Crundell (1) and S M Kinkead (6) |
| N5454 *HILDA* (coded '1') | 1 | 10 | R P Minifie |
| N6292 *LILY* | 8/1 | 10 | R R Soar (9), J H Winn (1) |
| N5444 *Canary Island Britons No 1* | 1 | 8 | T G Culling (6) and C A Eyre (2) |
| N5487 *BLACK PRINCE* | 10 | 8 | W M Alexander |
| N5440 *Britons in Siam No 1* | 1 | 7 | T F N Gerrard |
| N5460 | 8 | 7 | G G Simpson (5), J H Thompson (1) and C D Booker (1) |
| N5471 | 8 | 7 | R J O Compston |
| N6302 | 10 | 7 | G E Nash (1), A W Carter (4) and W M Alexander (2) |
| N6307 *BLACK DEATH* | 10 | 7 | J E Sharman |
| N6299 | 8/1 | 6 | R J O Compston (2) and S W Rosevear (4) |
| N5446 *Manaos Britons No 1* | 1 | 5 | R P Minifie |
| N5458 | 8/10 | 5 | A R Arnold (2) and D F FitzGibbon (3) |
| N5459 | 9/1 | 5 | O C LeBoutillier (4) and E W Desbarats (1) |
| N5469 | 8/9 | 5 | R A Little (4) and J C Tanner (1) |
| N5479 *Britons in Spain No 1* (coded '8') | 1 | 5 | Cockey (1), F H M Maynard (3) and J H Forman (1) |
| N5489 | 9/1 | 5 | E B Freeland (1) and S W Rosevear (4) |

# Triplanes Claimed by German Pilots (all in 1917)

| Date | Pilot | *Jasta* | Location | Time | Sqn | Serial | Victory number |
|---|---|---|---|---|---|---|---|
| 6 Apr | Hptm P Osterrhot | 12 | Henin-Lietard | 1215 | 1 | N5448 | 4 |
| 24 Apr | Ltn H Gontermann | 5 | Bailleul | 0900 | 8 | N5467 | 16 |
| 29 Apr | Rittm M v Richthofen | 11 | N Henin-Leitard | 1940 | 8 | N5441 | 52 |
| 1 May | Oblt K v Doring | 4 | NW Arleux | 1020 | 8 | N5434 | 2 |
| 1 May | Ltn K Wolff | 11 | S Seclin | 1050 | 8 | N5474 | 28 |
| 9 May | Vfw K Menckhoff | 3 | SW Farbus | 0850 | 8 | N5458 | 5 |
| 19 May | Oblt A v Tutschek | 12 | E Eterpigny | 0905 | 1 | N5461 | 9 |
| 19 May | Ltn G-W Groos | 11 | NW Izel | 2055 | 1 | N5488 | 1 |
| 23 May | OfStv P Aue | 10 | Carvin | 2115 | 8 | ? | unclear |
| 23 May | Ltn H Hintsch | 11 | Carvin | 2115 | 8 | N5481 | 3 |
| 24 May | Ltn O Maashoff | 11 | N Douai | 0902 | 8 | N5450 | 3 |
| 4 Jun | OfStv M Altemaier | 33 | St Leger | 0910 | 1 | u/c | 1 |
| 5 Jun | Ltn T Osterkamp | M1 | off Nieuport | ? | ? | Fr? | 3 |
| 8 Jun | Vzflugm Bossler | M1 | N Warneton | 1125 | 9 | N5491 | 1 |
| 8 Jun | OfStv M Müller | 28 | Quesnoy | 1910 | 1 | N6293 | 17 |
| 13 Jun | Uffz F Gille | 12 | St Laurent | 2105 | 1 | ? | 4 |
| 14 Jun | Vfw F Krebs | 6 | W Poezelhoek | 2030 | 10 | N5470 | 4 |
| 24 Jun | Ltn K Allmenröder | 11 | Polygon Wood | 0920 | 10 | N5358 | 28 |
| 24 Jun | Ltn G-W Groos | 11 | Keilergmolen | 0920 | 10 | N6306 | 2 |
| 25 Jun | Ltn K Allmenröder | 11 | W Quesnoy | 1845 | 10 | N5376 | 29 |
| 6 Jul | FlgMt B Heinrich | M1 | Reckem | 1650 | 1 | N5435 | 5 |

| Date | Pilot | *Jasta* | Location | Time | Sqn | Serial | Victory number |
|------|-------|---------|----------|------|-----|--------|----------------|
| 7 Jul | Ltn K Wolff | 11 | Comines | 1100 | 1 | N6309 | 33 |
| 7 Jul | Ltn R Krüger | 4 | W Wervicq | 1105 | 1 | N6291 | 1 |
| 7 Jul | Vfw F Altmeier | 24 | Bousebecque | 1105 | 1 | N5480 | 2 |
| 7 Jul | Ltn A Neiderhoff | 11 | Bousebecque | 1110 | 1 | N5480 | 4 |
| 11 Jul | Vfw J Buckler | 17 | SE Zillebeke | 0850 | 1 | N5357 | 8 (shared) |
| 11 Jul | Ltn H Bongartz | 36 | S Tenbrielen | 0900 | 1 | N5357 | 10 (shared) |
| 11 Jul | Ltn E Mohnicke | 11 | Comines | 2115 | 10 | N6304 | 3 |
| 11 Jul | Ltn W Blume | 26 | Comines | 2100 | 10 | N6304 | 3 |
| 12 Jul | Ltn W Güttler | 24 | Klein Zillebeke | 0850 | 10 | N5368 | 3 |
| 12 Jul | Ltn A Hübner | 4 | Zuidschute | 2120 | 10 | N5364 | unclear |
| 20 Jul | Ltn A Neiderhoff | 11 | Zonnebeke | 2110 | 10 | N5429 | 6 (shared) |
| 20 Jul | Vfw K Wüsthoff | 4 | SW Becelaere | 2120 | 10 | N5429 | 5 (shared) |
| 22 Jul | Ltn O Brauneck | 11 | Becelaere | 1125 | 10 | N5478 | 10 |
| 24 Jul | Ltn H Dilthey | 27 | Passchendaele | 2015 | 10 | N5364 | 1 |
| 27 Jul | Ltn K-A v Schönebeck | 11 | Beythem | 2040 | 10 | N5492 | 1 |
| 28 Jul | Oblt A v Tutschek | 12 | Mericourt | 0730 | 8 | N5493 | 19 |
| 31 Jul | Uffz K Reinhold | 24 | Bailleul | 1630 | ? | ? | 1 |
| 9 Aug | Ltn W Güttler | 24 | E Dixmude | 0910 | 10 | N6290 | 4 |
| 11 Aug | Ltn V Schobinger | 12 | Farbus | 2040 | 8 | N5482 | 2 |
| 12 Aug | Ltn H Kroll | 24 | N Ypres | 0900 | ? | ? | 7 |
| 14 Aug | Uffz K Steudel | 3 | Langemarck | 1720 | 10 | N536 | 3 |
| 16 Aug | Ltn G-W Groos | 11 | Hollebeke | 1120 | 1 | N6304 | 4 |
| 20 Aug | Vfw R Heibert | 33 | NE Dixmude | 0855 | 0 | ? | 1 |
| 20 Aug | Ltn J Jacobs | 7 | Langemarck | 1735 | 10 | N5355 | 6 |
| 21 Aug | Ltn E Hess | 28 | Ypres | 1840 | 10 | N5425 | unclear |
| 21 Aug | Hptm O Hartmann | 28 | E Becelaere | 1935 | 1 | N6308 | 7 |
| 21 Aug | Ltn J Schmidt | 3 | ? | ? | ? | ? | unclear |
| 23 Aug | Oblt O v Boenigk | 4 | Boesinghe | 0905 | ? | ? | 3 |
| 25 Aug | Ltn H G v d Osten | 11 | Langemarck | 0855 | 10 | N5367 | 2 |
| 3 Sep | Ltn K Hammes | 35 | SE Essen | 0955 | Fr | N5388 | 3 |
| 3 Sep | Ltn K-A v Schönebeck | 11 | E Hollebeke | 1005 | 1 | N5381 | 3 (shared) |
| 3 Sep | Ltn E Stapenhorst | 11 | Wytschaete | 1030 | 1 | N5381 | 2 (shared) |
| 9 Sep | Ltn H Kroll | 24 | NE Zillebeke | 1835 | 1 | N5477 | 9 |
| 11 Sep | Ltn H Kroll | 24 | Bellewaarde | 0945 | ? | ? | unclear |
| 13 Sep | Ltn K Wüsthoff | 4 | S Wervicq | 0830 | 1 | N5429 | 15 |
| 19 Sep | Vfw F Kosmahl | 26 | Passchendaele | 1755 | 1 | N5490 | 8 |
| 20 Sep | Ltn K Stock | 6 | Kemmel | 0950 | 1 | ? | 1 |
| 20 Sep | Ltn R Wendelmuth | 8 | N Passchendaele | 0950 | 1 | N6292 | 8 |
| 20 Sep | Vfw F Kosmahl | 26 | Passchendaele | 1150 | 1 | N5459 | 9 |
| 26 Sep | Vfw M Wackwitz | 24 | SE Linselles | ? | 1Fr | ? | 3 |
| 26 Sep | Vfw F Altemeier | 24 | W Comines | ? | 1Fr | ? | 8 |
| 26 Sep | Ltn T Quandt | 36 | Passchendaele | 1210 | 1 | N5440 | 5 |
| 26 Sep | Ltn H Bongartz | 36 | Houthulst | ? | 1 | N5421 | 12 |
| 5 Oct | Ltn Wilde | 4 | Dadizeele | 0750 | 1 | N5377 | 1 |
| 9 Oct | Ltn K Gallwitz | 2 | N Zevekote | 1815 | ? | ? | 3 |
| 12 Oct | Vfw K Menckhoff | 3 | Zonnebeke | 1020 | ? | ? | 13 |
| 24 Oct | Ltn W Blume | 26 | Tenbrielen | 1250 | 1 | N5476 | 5 |
| 27 Oct | Ltn K Wüsthoff | 4 | Hooge | 0930 | 1 | N5455 | 22 |

# Triplanes serving with the French Navy

| French Serial | Fuselage number | British Serial[14] | French/British Service |
|---|---|---|---|
| F1 | '9' | - | 11/12/16 to 22/4/17[1] |
| F2 | '12' | - | 11/12/16 to 21/4/17[2] |
| F3 | '10' | - | 15/1/17 to 7/17 |
| F4 | '4' | - | 11/12/16 to 14/1/17[3] |
| F5 | '11' | N541 | 30/12/16 to 8/11/17 |
| F6 | '15' | N5388 | 14/2/17 to 7/17 |
| F7 | '13' | - | 29/1/17 to 17/7/17[4] |
| F8 | '17' | - | 1/3/17 to 27/6/17[5] |
| F9 | '14' | N542 | 2/2/17 to 1/11/17[6] |
| F10 | '16' | N543 | 1/03/17 to 8/11/17[7] |
| F11 | '9' | N5384 | 23/6/17 to 11/10/17[8] |
| F12 | '12' | N5385 | 23/6/17 to 13/7/17[9] |
| F13 | ? | N5386 | 24/6/17 to 11/10/17[10] |
| F14 | ? | N5387 | 24/6/17 to 11/10/17[11] |
| F15 | '13' | - | 21/7/17 to 3/9/17[12] |
| F16 | ? | - | 21/7/17 to ? |
| ? | ? | N524 | 28/3/17-4/17[13] |

## Notes

(1)     Destroyed in a landing accident on 22 April 1917

(2)     Destroyed in a landing accident on 21 April 1917

(3)     Crashed on take-off on 14 January 1917 and written off

(4)     Destroyed in forced landing on 17 July 1917

(5)     Destroyed in a collision with an RNAS aircraft on 27 June 1917

(6)     Transferred to RNAS on 2 November 1917

(7)     Transferred to RNAS on 8 November 1917

(8)     Transferred to RNAS on 11 October 1917

(9)     Destroyed in accident on 13 July 1917, pilot H Barbier killed

(10)    Transferred to RNAS on 11 October 1917

(11)    Transferred to RNAS on 11 October 1917

(12)    Shot down in combat on 3 September 1917, pilot H Le Garrec killed

(13)    Purchased back from French government in April 1917. Fuselage number not known. Obviously this Triplane had not been with the French for very long, and may not have had either an F number or a fuselage number allocated

(14)    British serial numbers allocated when machines returned to RNAS service

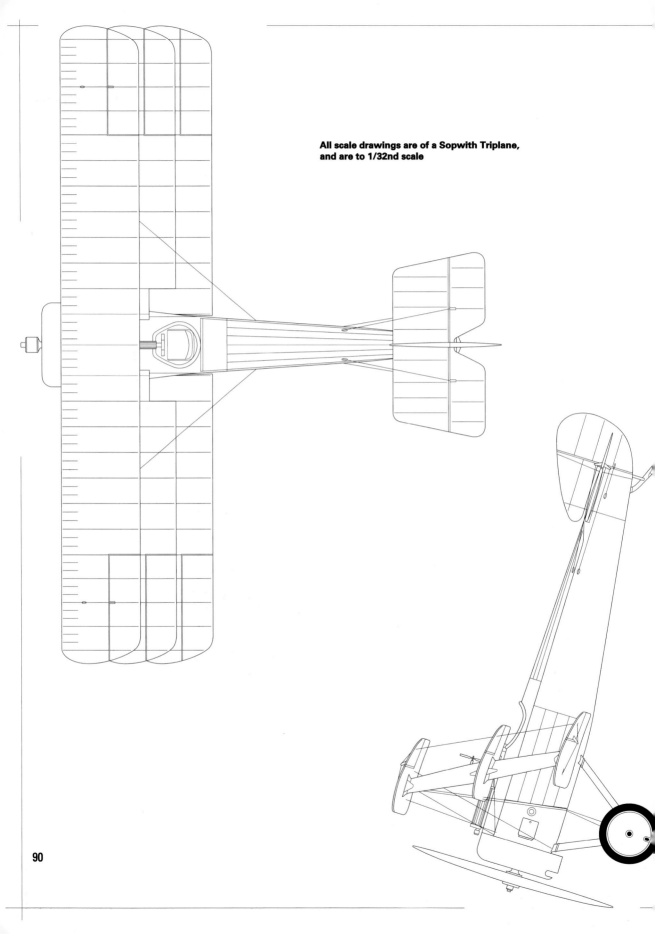

**All scale drawings are of a Sopwith Triplane, and are to 1/32nd scale**

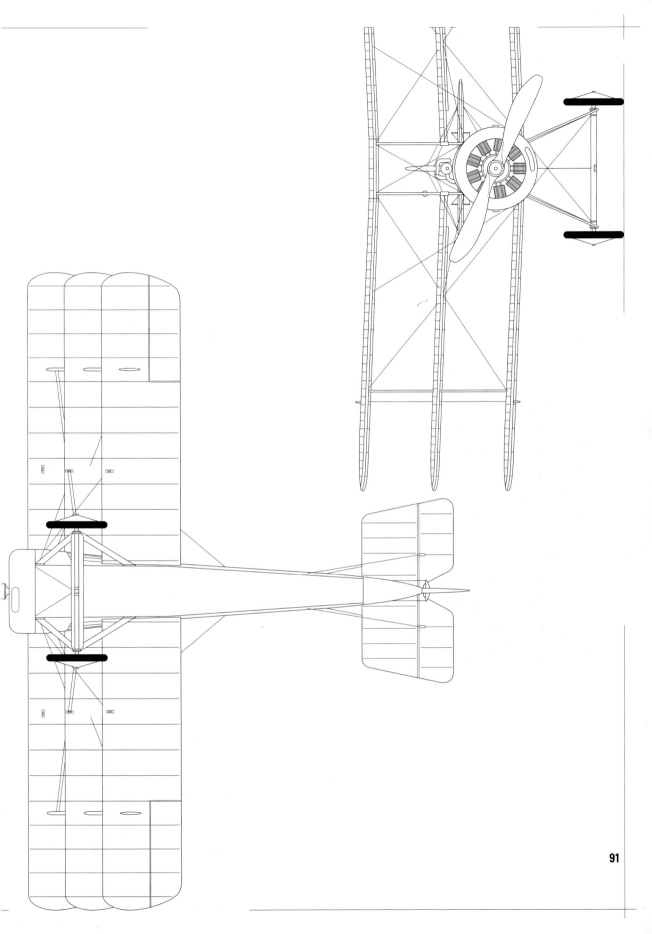

# COLOUR PLATES

## 1

**Prototype Triplane N500, 'A' Naval Squadron, 1 Naval Wing, Furnes, Belgium, July 1916**

The aircraft was flown by the squadron in order to evaluate the new Sopwith scout under combat conditions. It arrived in Belgium in clear-doped factory finish, with a natural metal cowling and no serial number on the fuselage. Future ace R S Dallas scored at least two combat victories with it, and most 'A' Squadron pilots flew the fighter so as to gain experience on type.

## 2

**Prototype Triplane N500 *BROWN BREAD*, 'A' Naval Squadron, 1 Naval Wing, Furnes, Belgium, late 1916**

Now camouflaged in British PC12 khaki (almost a chocolate brown colour), with clear-doped undersides, the Triplane prototype now displays its serial in black, edged in white. The name *BROWN BREAD*, painted on the fuselage sides beneath the cockpit, refers to its overall colour, and has nothing to do with cockney rhyming slang.

## 3

**Triplane N5454 'I', 1 Naval Squadron, Bailleul, France, October 1917**

This machine was used by 1 Naval Squadron's second-ranking Triplane ace, Australian R P Minifie, to achieve ten of his victories. The unit identification marking of two small white bars on the fuselage sides aft of the number '1' was introduced in August 1917. Its cowling was camouflaged and its wheel covers were red, as was the tail fin, denoting the scout's assignment to 'A' Flight.

## 4

**Triplane N5387 '15' *PEGGY.*, 1 Naval Squadron, Bailleul, France, August 1917**

This aircraft also displayed a camouflaged engine cowling, although its wheel covers and fin were painted white. The fighter had previously been operated by French naval pilots, as F14, at St Pol, and was at one time flown by the famous French ace Charles Nungesser.

## 5

**Triplane N5436 'C', 1 Naval Squadron, La Bellevue, France, April 1917**

Australian ace R S Dallas of 'Naval 1' flew this aircraft between December 1916 and May 1917, during which time he used it to claim 11 victories. Future ace C B Ridley then flew the veteran fighter in August and September 1917, scoring a further two victories with it. Very much a 'plain Jane' Triplane, it had a metal cowling and a clear-doped fin and wheel covers.

## 6

**Triplane N6303, Home Defence, Chingford, Essex, June 1917**

This aircraft served initially with 10 Naval Squadron (where it was flown by high-scoring ace E V Reid) and then went to 1 Naval Squadron in July 1917, where it became R P Minifie's mount until mid-August. He claimed two of his victories with the fighter during the course of 34 patrols. Eventually damaged in a forced landing, N6303 returned to the squadron for use by other pilots after repairs had been effected, only for it to be 'pranged' in a second forced landing on 20 September. Featuring a camouflaged cowling and white wheel covers, but without any distinguishing unit markings, this is how the machine looked at Chingford in 1918.

## 7

**Triplane N5479 '8' (presentation machine *Britons of Spain No 1*), 1 Naval Squadron, Bailleul, France, June 1917**

F H M Maynard claimed three of his six Triplane victories while flying this aircraft, and L H Cockey and J H Forman each added another to take the machine's total to five. This aircraft displays the original serial presentation on the fuselage, the number being applied in white. Later, the RNAS standardised on black letter/numbers being applied on a white rectangle. N5479 has a camouflaged cowling and a white fin and wheel covers.

## 8

**Triplane N5427 '13' ( presentation machine *Philippine Island Britons No1*), 1 Naval Squadron, La Bellevue, France, April 1917**

F H M Maynard was flying this machine on Christmas Eve 1916 when he claimed a victory. By July 1917 the scout was serving with 'Naval 8', after which it joined 'Naval 9', before being retired in August. It too has a camouflaged cowling and a white fin and wheel covers.

## 9

**Triplane N5437 '14', 1 Naval Squadron, Bailleul, France, April 1917**

C B Ridley gained his first victory with this aircraft on 29 April 1917. R S Dallas also flew it, and H Day claimed his one and only Triplane kill with N5437 on 12 August. Four days later, J A Cole claimed this machine's third victory. The fighter's serial has been painted directly onto the fuselage, and it displays a camouflaged cowling and a white fin and wheel covers.

## 10

**Triplane N534 'F', 1 Naval Squadron, Bailleul, France, July 1917**

Used by high-scoring 'Naval 1' aces Dallas, Minifie and Maynard (all of whom gained a single kill with it), N534 was one of the few two-gun Triplanes to reach the frontline. Unusually, it displays two large white fuselage bands and two smaller ones on the rear wing and elevators. A stylised 'F' is painted on the Triplane's all black fin, and it has a camouflaged cowling and wheel covers.

## 11

**Triplane N5472 '17', 1 Naval Squadron, Bailleul, France, October 1917**

This aircraft had previously served with both 8 and 9 Naval Squadrons prior to its allocation to 'Naval 1' in the autumn of 1917. It had been used by ace R McDonald to claim one of his three Triplane kills during the scout's spell with 'Naval 8', and nine-kill ace H V Rowley claimed his fifth, and last, Triplane victory with N5472 on 13 November 1917. Fitted with a pointed propeller boss, this aircraft has standard 'Naval 1' unit markings of two vertical white bars, as well as a white fin and wheel covers

## 12

### Triplane N5377 '4', 1 Naval Squadron, 1 Naval Squadron, Bailleul, France, 5 October 1917

This aircraft, previously operated by 9 Naval Squadron, is also marked with two white vertical bars in accordance with the unit's post-August 1917 squadron scheme. It also displays the numeral '4', which is repeated on the top fuselage deck-ing, as well as a red fin and wheel covers. E Pierce of 9 Naval Squadron scored one victory with the machine on 17 July 1917 and 1 Naval Squadron's future five-kill ace F J W Mellersh used it to share a victory on 28 July – his solitary claim with the Triplane. N5377 was lost on the morning of 5 October in combat with *Jasta* 4's Ltn Wilde over Dadizeele, M J Watson being shot down and captured.

## 13

### Triplane N5454 *HILDA*, 8 Naval Squadron, Furnes, Belgium, March 1917

Ace R R Soar named this aircraft after his cousin. According to his log-book, he flew this machine from 1 through to 17 March 1917, when it then went to 9 Naval Squadron and then 1 Naval (see profile 3). Soar was flying this machine on 1 March when he engaged a Gotha which had just bombed Broadstairs, in Kent. The Triplane has a metal cowling and a white fin and wheel covers, with the name appearing on both sides of the fuselage.

## 14

### Triplane N5482 *MAUD*, 8 Naval Squadron, St-Eloi, France, May-August 1917

C D Booker used this aircraft as his personal mount, achieving 17 victories with it between April and August 1917. N5482 has a metal cowling, blue fin and wheel covers with the name *MAUD* displayed below the cockpit. Personal markings also extended to a highly unusual red, white and blue zig-zag pat-tern around the fuselage. The scout also has a pointed pro-peller boss. This machine was lost after a successful combat on 11 August, and although Booker survived the forced-landing, the machine was subsequently destroyed by an artillery barrage.

## 15

### Triplane N5493 *BLYMP*, 8 Naval Squadron, St-Eloi, France, May-July 1917

Ranking Australian ace R A Little achieved 20 victories in this machine between April and July 1917, making it the second most successful Triplane in aerial combat after Ray Collishaw's N5492. It has a metal cowling and white fin and wheel covers, with Little's nickname for his young son appearing below the cockpit on both sides of the fuselage. A red vertical band, edged in white, circles the fuselage, with a dagger-like pattern on the top decking. The aircraft was badly shot up in combat while being flown by future ace E D Crundall on 28 July. Once repaired (and now no longer flown by Little), N5493 had a red heart added to the fuselage sides and the name deleted, while the red band was extended on the top decking to form a dagger motif. On 6 September

N5493 was destroyed in a mid-air collision with a No 19 Sqn SPAD VII.

## 16

### Triplane N5468 *ANGEL*, 8 Naval Squadron, St-Eloi, France, June 1917

C H B Jenner-Parsons claimed at least two victories while flying this machine, which had a metal cowling and a clear-doped fin and wheel covers. The scout had logged 178 flying hours by the time it was sent to 12 Naval Squadron (the RNAS's dedicated training unit) at Hondschoote, in Belgium, at the end of 1917.

## 17

### Triplane N5465, 8 Naval Squadron, St-Eloi, France, April-June 1917

Future nine-kill ace R R Thornely scored three victories, and possibly two more, while flying this aircraft, and E D Crundall used it to claim a solitary kill as well. Passed on to 'Naval 1', N5465 enjoyed further success with 35-kill ace S M Kinkead at the controls, the South African claiming all six of his Triplane victories in the aircraft between 17 September and 12 November 1917. Devoid of any fuselage markings, the scout has a metal cowling and a blue fin and wheel covers. The serial number has been applied in white directly onto the fuselage canvas.

## 18

### Triplane N5421 *High Jinks*, 8 Naval Squadron, St-Eloi, France, August 1917

Future Camel ace W L Jordon damaged this machine in a dusk landing on 5 June 1917, and following repairs nine-kill ace R B Munday used it to gain his sole Triplane victory. N5421 later served with 'Naval 1' until it was shot down by *Jasta* 36's 33-kill ace Ltn Heinrich Bongartz on 26 September 1917, its pilot being taken prisoner. While serving with '8 Naval', the scout featured the white squadron circle/disc marking aft of the fuselage roundel, while its serial number was painted directly onto the fuselage. Note its camouflaged fin and wheel covers.

## 19

### Triplane N5449 *BINKY III*, 8 Naval Squadron, St-Eloi, France, May 1917

This machine bore two names – *JOAN* and then *BINKY III*. Aces P A Johnston, E D Crundall and A G A Spence used the aircraft on various occasions, the last-named after it had been passed to 'Naval 1' in September. It was subsequently numbered '13' (previously allocated to N5427). Unusually, N5549 was flown in the frontline with the full Sopwith titling and place of manufacture details still stencilled onto its clear-doped fin.

## 20

### Triplane N6301 *DUSTY II*, 8 Naval Squadron, St-Eloi, France, May 1917

R McDonald flew this aircraft, which moved between 8 and 10 Naval Squadrons before finally going to 1 Naval Squadron, where aces F H M Maynard and H V Rowley flew it on occasion. The veteran scout was eventually destroyed by fire at 'Naval 1's' Bailleul home on the night of 1 October 1917.

Aside from N6301's red and white fuselage stripe, the Triplane also displays a camouflaged cowling and wheel covers, but a clear-doped fin.

## 21

### Triplane N6290 *DIXIE*, 8 Naval Squadron, St-Eloi, France, May-June 1917

This aircraft fell victim to *Jasta* 24's Ltn W Güttler on 9 August 1917, its pilot, K R Munro, being killed in the action. It had previously been flown by aces P A Johnston in May and A R Arnold in June. The scout displays a fuselage band similar to that which adorned Bob Little's aircraft, although with reversed colours of white, with red and white edging. This band was extended along the top of the fuselage in a dagger-style marking. At some stage the Triplane became *DIXIE II*, when two small white vertical bars were added under the name below the cockpit. The cowling and wheel covers are camouflaged. On 10 April 1992 a replica Triplane numbered N6290, but with a white fin bearing a red circle, was flown by the Shuttleworth Collection in Bedfordshire, the fighter being registered as G-BOCK. This machine was deemed to be such a perfect reproduction by none other than 'Tommy' Sopwith himself that it was given a company production number by the great man just prior to his death.

## 22

### Triplane N5459, 9 Naval Squadron, Flez, France, June 1917

American O C 'Boots' LeBoutillier scored three of his four Triplane victories while flying this aircraft, which had earlier served with 'Naval 1' until it was damaged in collision with an RE 8 on 20 April. Following its return to 1 Naval Squadron in August, E W Desbarats claimed a single victory with the aircraft, but was then himself shot down by *Jasta* 26's Vfw F Kosmahl for his ninth kill (and his second Triplane in two days) on 20 September – Desbarats was taken prisoner. The scout has a metal cowling and white wheel covers, as well as a diagonal red and white fuselage stripe.

## 23

### Triplane '10', *Centre d'Aviation Maritime*, Dunkirk, France, April 1917

French aircraft were painted in British PC12 khaki, with metal cowlings and clear-doped wheel covers. Individual aircraft displayed numbers just ahead of the fuselage roundel, and this was repeated on the top fuselage decking. Pierre Malvoisin used machines marked '10' and '11' in 1917, and engaged in several combats – he used this machine to intercept an Albatros two-seater on 12 April.

## 24

### Triplane N5431, 2 Naval Wing, Mudros, eastern Mediterranean, November 1917

This was the sole Triplane to see service in the eastern Mediterranean, having been sent to the Mudros, on the Greek island of Lemnos, for rebuilding after it was badly damaged in an accident at Mikra Bay airfield near Salonika on 26 March 1917. At one stage it was coded 'L', although most photographs do not support this. Once rebuilt, the aircraft was flown by H T Mellings, who gained four victories in it. The scout had a metal cowling and clear-doped wheel covers

but apparently no serial was applied after its rebuild. Note the additional Lewis gun mounting.

## 25

### Triplane N5382 *THE OOSLUMBURD*, Manston War Flight (Home Defence), Manston, Kent, July 1917

Displaying the odd nickname *THE OOSLUMBURD* below its cockpit, this aircraft was used by future seven-kill ace Rowan Daly to engage raiding Gotha bombers over the south coast on 7 July 1917. Aside from the name, this Triplane is conventionally marked with a metal cowling and clear-doped wheel covers.

## 26

### Triplane N5492 *BLACK MARIA*, 10 Naval Squadron, Droglandt, France, June-July 1917

The highest-scoring Triplane of them all, N5492 was credited with no fewer than 23 kills. Eighteen of these were scored by Raymond Collishaw, leader of 'Naval 10's' 'B' Flight, which was known as the 'Black Flight' because its aircraft had black-painted cowlings and bore names starting with the word 'Black'. Collishaw's had the name *BLACK MARIA* painted below the cockpit of his aircraft, while the serial number N5492 was applied in white directly onto the fuselage. The scout's wheel covers were also painted black. G E Nash later scored a further five victories with this outstandingly successful aircraft.

## 27

### Triplane N533 'C' *'BLACK MARIA'*, 10 Naval Squadron, Droglandt, France, June-July 1917

Another of Collishaw's machines, this aircraft also displays a large letter 'C' aft of the fuselage roundel, which was repeated on the uppersurface of the starboard rear elevator. The cowling has again been painted black, as have the fin and wheel covers. On 27 July 1917 Collishaw achieved two victories in this machine, which was one of only a handful of Triplanes armed with twin Vickers guns. Various published sources report as few as six 'Tripes' (Clayton & Shuttleworth-built machines N533 to N538) received the two-gun fit.

## 28

### Triplane N5487 'A' *BLACK PRINCE*, 10 Naval Squadron, Droglandt, France, June-July 1917

W M Alexander scored eight of his ten Triplane victories in this aircraft during the summer of 1917. Like all 'B' Flight aircraft, its cowling and wheel covers were painted black. The scout's serial number was applied directly onto the fuselage canvas.

## 29

### Triplane N5483 'R' *BLACK ROGER*, 10 Naval Squadron, Droglandt, France, June-July 1917

'Black' Flight pilot E V Reid claimed 17 victories with this Triplane in June and July 1917, but failed to return from a patrol in it on 28 July (he had scored his 17th victory during the course of his final sortie). Reid's aircraft had been hit by shells fired from *K Flak* Unit 21. Exhibiting standard 'B' Flight colours, the fighter was appropriately marked with the letter 'R' for Reid.

## 30
### Triplane N5376 'N' *BLACK SHEEP,* 10 Naval Squadron, Droglandt, France, June 1917

On 25 June 1917, G E Nash was flying this aircraft when he was shot down by Karl Allmenröder of *Jasta* 11 – this was the German ace's second Triplane kill in two days, and it represented his 29th victory overall. Nash was wounded and taken prisoner. As previously mentioned, five of his six kills were scored flying Collishaw's 'old' Triplane N5492 during May and June 1917. It is not known whether the latter machine had a white 'N' added to its fuselage after it was passed onto Nash.

## 31
### Triplane N6307 'S' *BLACK DEATH,* 10 Naval Squadron, Droglandt, France, June-July 1917

J E Sharman used this machine to claim six of his seven Triplane victories in June and July 1917. As with other aircraft in the squadron at the time, the scout features the initial letter of the pilot's surname behind the fuselage roundel. It was perhaps an unfortunate name for Sharman to choose for his Triplane as he met his own death while flying N6307 on 22 July. Like squadronmate G E Nash, he was brought down by a burst of well-aimed flak, fired this time by *Flak Batterie* 503.

## 32
### Triplane N5366, 10 Naval Squadron, Droglandt, France, June-July 1917

J E Sharman, G L Trapp and H W Taylor flew this aircraft in combat, and each used it to gain one victory. N5366 then went to 8 Naval Squadron, where it was damaged in a collision on 5 September. Following repair, it ended its days with No 204 Training Depot Station in Eastchurch, in Kent. The front section of the aircraft's metal cowling is painted red, as is the fin and wheel covers (thus denoting its assignment to 'A' Flight), whilst the serial has been applied within a rectangle of white paint.

## 33
### Triplane N5359 'P', 10 Naval Squadron, Droglandt, France, June 1917

Flown by J A Page, this machine displays 'C' Flight's blue marking in abundance in the form of a suitably decorated cowling, fin and wheel covers. The serial number was white, painted directly onto the fuselage. Page claimed four victories with this machine in June 1917.

## 34
### Triplane N6295 'B', 10 Naval Squadron, Droglandt, France, August 1917

After being used by W M Alexander, this aircraft became the personal machine of Flt Cdr H J T Saint. He used it to claim two victories in late August 1917, having been slightly wounded while flying the fighter a few days early on the 16th. N6295 was duly passed onto 'Naval 1' when 'Naval 10' completed its re-equipment with Camels in September 1917. The Triplane's letter code 'B' was a hangover from its first assigned pilot, Canadian S Broughall.

## 35
### Triplane N5429 '2', 1 Naval Squadron, Bailleul, France, September 1917

Previously serving as with both 10 and 8 Naval Squadrons,

this machine was shot down by Kurt Wüsthoff (for his 15th victory) on 13 September 1917. Its pilot, Flt Sub-Lt J R Wilford, was captured. Whilst with 'Naval 10', this machine had been been credited with two kills at the hands of H W Taylor. The scout's serial number had been stencilled directly onto the fuselage, and also note its pointed propeller boss.

## 36
### Triplane N5429 now in German markings, France, September 1917

Captured virtually intact after being shot up by *Jasta* 4's 27-victory ace Kurt Wüsthoff, 'Naval 1's N5429 soon had its tailfin and rudder painted white, and the white '2' obscured by a German cross. Finally, the unit's white vertical bars were also painted out.

# INDEX

References to illustrations are shown in **bold**. Plates are shown with page and caption locators in brackets.